Premier &
EFL Football Supporter's
Guide & Yearbook
2025

EDITOR
John Robinson

Thirty-ninth Edition

CONTENTS

British Library Cataloguing in Publication Data
A catalogue record for this book is available from the British Library

ISBN: 978-1-86223-522-9

Copyright © 2024, SOCCER BOOKS LIMITED (01472 696226)
72 St. Peter's Avenue, Cleethorpes, DN35 8HU, United Kingdom
Website   www.soccer-books.co.uk
e-mail   info@soccer-books.co.uk

Printed in the UK by 4edge Ltd

FOREWORD

Following last year's re-launch of our 'Supporters' Guide' series of books in October 2023, we are glad to be able to publish all three fully-updated guides in time for the start of the 2024-2025 football season

Please note that, as matches are often catergorised with different admission prices dependant upon the opposition, where possible we have shown the range payable on the matchdays themselves although, in the event of clubs operating dynamic pricing policies, differences may apply. Many clubs offer a discount for advance ticket purchases (which is usually around £2.00 for each ticket).

For a number of clubs, particularly those in the Premier League and EFL Championship, the availability of Matchday tickets is very low and, where this is the case we have been unable to show the normal price range at all. Also, where matchday admission prices for the 2024-2025 season had not been announced when we went to press, we have shown the prices used by the clubs for the previous season.

We are indebted to the staffs of all the clubs featured in this guide for their cooperation and also to Michael Robinson (page layouts), Bob Budd (cover artwork) and Tony Brown (Cup Statistics – www.soccerdata.com).

Separate information for Disabled Supporters is once again included in the guide and, to ensure that facilities are not overstretched, we recommend that fans with disabilities pre-book because suitable seating and parking facilities are likely to be restricted.

Finally, we would like to wish our readers a safe spectating season.

John Robinson
EDITOR

WEMBLEY STADIUM

First Opened: 1923 (Re-opened in 2007 after rebuild)
Address: Wembley National Stadium, Wembley, London HA9 0WS
Correspondence: P.O.Box 1966, London, SW1P 3EQ
Telephone N°: 0844 980-8001 or 0800 169-2007
Stadium Tours: 0800 169-9933

Seating Capacity: 90,000 over three tiers –
Lower Tier: 34,303 seats
Middle Tier: 16,532 seats
Upper Tier: 39,165 seats
Modern Era Record Attendance: 89,874 (2008)
Website: www.wembleystadium.com

GENERAL INFORMATION

Car Parking: The stadium is a Public Transport Location and, as such, parking is only available for pre-accredited vehicles. Any spaces which are available must be pre-purchased from the following website: www.wembleyofficialparking.com

Coach Travel: National Express operates coach routes from hundreds of towns and cities direct to the stadium for special events: www.nationalexpress.com/wembley

Rail & Tube Travel: Wembley Park station is on the Jubilee and Metropolitan tube lines; Wembley Stadium station is on the Chiltern mainline and Wembley Central station is served by the Bakerloo tube, London Overground and London Midland and Southern railway lines.

Local Bus Services: Services 83, 92 and 224 all travel to the stadium

FANS WITH DISABILITIES INFORMATION

Wheelchairs: 310 spaces for wheelchairs are available in total alongside 310 seats for helpers. A further 100 enhanced amenity seats are available for ambulant visitors. 26 lifts around the stadium assist with access.

Disabled Toilets: 147 toilets are available throughout the stadium with access via the Radar Key system.

Contact: For information and assistance contact the Disability liaison officer on 0800 169-2007 (Option 7) or E-mail pod@wembleystadium.com

PREMIER LEAGUE

Website   www.premierleague.com

E-mail   info@premierleague.com

Clubs for the 2024/2025 Season

AFC BOURNEMOUTH

Founded: 1899 (**Entered League**: 1923)
Former Names: Boscombe FC (1899-1923);
Bournemouth & Boscombe Athletic FC (1923-1972)
Nickname: 'Cherries'
Ground: Vitality Stadium, Dean Court,
Bournemouth, Dorset   BH7 7AF
Ground Capacity: 11,364 (All seats)

Record Attendance: 11,772 (21st July 2013)
Colours: Red & Black striped shirts with Black shorts
Telephone Nº & Ticket Office Nº: (01202) 726300
Website: www.afcb.co.uk
E-mail: enquiries@afcb.co.uk

GENERAL INFORMATION

Car Parking: Car Park for 200 cars behind the ground and free parking is available at Harewood College (10 mins. walk)
Coach Parking: At the ground
Nearest Railway Station: Bournemouth Central (1½ miles)
Nearest Bus Stop: Holdenhurst Road, Bournemouth
Club Shop: At the ground
Opening Times: Monday to Friday 9.00am to 5.00pm, Saturday 9.30am to 4.00pm, Sunday 10.00am to 3.00pm and Saturday Matchdays 9.00am to kick-off + 30 minutes after the final whistle.
Telephone Nº: (01202) 726300

GROUND INFORMATION

Away Supporters' Entrances & Sections:
East Stand turnstiles 'F' 14-16 for East Stand accommodation

ADMISSION INFO (2024/2025 PRICES)

Note: Because of the limited capacity at the Vitality Stadium, Dean Court, most seats for 2024/2025 will be taken by season ticket holders so please contact the club for any further information.

FANS WITH DISABILITIES INFORMATION

Wheelchairs: Spaces available in all stands
Helpers: One carer admitted per fan with disabilities
Prices: £5.00 for those in wheelchairs.
Disabled Toilets: Available in the Main Stand, East Stand and North Stand
E-mail Contact: disability@afcb.co.uk

Travelling Supporters' Information: Routes: From the North & East: Take the A338 into Bournemouth and turn left at 'Kings Park' turning. After the slip road go straight forward at the mini-roundabout into Kings Park Drive – a car park is 500 yards on the left and the ground is nearby; From the West: Head into Bournemouth and join the A338, take the slip road at the Springbourne Roundabout, signposted for Kings Park. Take the 3rd exit at the roundabout at the fire station, stay in the left-hand lane and turn left onto Holdenhurst Road. Go straight on at the traffic lights (the Queen's Park Pub should be on the right) and take the 3rd exit at the mini roundabout into Kings Park for the ground.

ARSENAL FC

Founded: 1886 (**Entered League**: 1893)	**Record Attendance**: 60,383 (2nd November 2019)
Former Names: Royal Arsenal (1886-1891) and Woolwich Arsenal (1891-1914)	**Colours**: Red shirts with White sleeves, White shorts
Nickname: 'Gunners'	**Telephone N°**: (020) 7619-5003
Ground: Emirates Stadium, Hornsey Road, London, N7 7AJ	**Office Address**: Highbury House, 75 Drayton Park, London N5 1BU
Ground Capacity: 60,704 (All seats)	**Website**: www.arsenal.com
	E-mail: via 'contact us' on website

GENERAL INFORMATION

Car Parking: None
Coach Parking: Visit the website for further details
Nearest Railway Station: Finsbury Park and Highbury & Islington
Nearest Tube Station: Arsenal (Piccadilly), Finsbury Park, Highbury & Islington and Holloway Road are all nearby
Club Shop: At the ground and at Finsbury Park Tube Station
Opening Times: Monday to Saturday 9.00am to 6.00pm; Sundays 10.00am to 4.00pm (9.00am to 6.00pm at Finsbury Park)
Telephone N°: (020) 7619-5000

GROUND INFORMATION

Away Supporters' Entrances & Sections:
Green quadrant in the south east corner of the ground – follow colour coding system at the ground

ADMISSION INFO (2024/2025 PRICES)

Adult Seating: £34.00 – £141.00
Child Seating: £21.30 – £40.90 (Members only)
Senior Citizen Seating: £22.73 – £55.73 (Members only)
Young Adults Seating: £35.93 – £105.75 (Members only)
Note: Prices vary depending on the category of the game. Concessionary prices are only available to Members.

FANS WITH DISABILITIES INFORMATION

Wheelchairs: 250 spaces available in areas throughout the ground. A similar number of places are available for the ambulant and visually impaired
Helpers: One helper admitted for each fan with disabilities
Prices: £15.15 – £37.15. Helpers are admitted free
Disabled Toilets: Many available throughout the ground
Free commentaries are available for the visually impaired
Contact: (020) 7619-5050 (Bookings are necessary) – Details on club website via 'Club' main heading

Travelling Supporters' Information:
As the stadium is situated in a mainly residential area, only car owners with resident's permits will be allowed to park in the designated on-street parking areas. Cars parked illegally will be towed away so use public transport whenever possible. The nearest tube station is Arsenal (Piccadilly Line) which is 3 minutes walk from the ground with Finsbury Park (Victoria & Piccadilly Lines) and Highbury & Islington about 10 minutes walk away.

ASTON VILLA FC

Photo courtesy of Neville Williams/Aston Villa FC

Founded: 1874 (**Entered League**: 1888)
Former Names: None
Nicknames: 'The Villans' 'Villa'
Ground: Villa Park, Trinity Road, Birmingham B6 6HE
Ground Capacity: 42,095 (All seats)
Record Attendance: 76,588 (2nd March 1946)

Colours: Claret shirts with Blue sleeves, White shorts
Telephone N°: (0121) 327-2299
Ticket Office: 0333 323-1874
Consumer Sales: 0330 053-6010
Website: www.avfc.co.uk
E-mail: postmaster@avfc.co.uk

GENERAL INFORMATION

Ground Tours: 0333 323-1874
Car Parking: Stadium Car Park (permit only on matchdays) or street parking away from the ground
Away Coach Parking: Opposite the ground on Witton Lane
Nearest Railway Station: Witton or Aston (5 mins. walk)
Nearest Bus Station: Birmingham Centre
Club Shop: 'Villa Village' at the ground
Opening Times: Villa Village: Monday to Saturday 10.00am to 5.00pm (9.00am on Saturday) & Sunday 10.00am to 4.00pm.
Telephone N°: 0330 053-6010

GROUND INFORMATION

Away Supporters' Entrances & Sections:
Doug Ellis Stand – Blocks 'P' & 'Q'

ADMISSION INFO (2024/2025 PRICES)

Adult Seating: £30.00 – £51.00
Concessionary Seating: £27.50 – £36.50
Under-21s Seating: £27.50 – £29.50
Under-18s Seating: £21.50 – £23.00
Under-14s Seating: £15.50 – £16.50 (Under-14s must be accompanied by a paying adult to attend matches)

FANS WITH DISABILITIES INFORMATION

Wheelchairs: 87 spaces in total in the Trinity Road Stand lower, 8 of which are for away supporters
Helpers: Admitted on request – one per fan with disabilities
Prices: Normal prices for fans with disabilities, helpers free
Disabled Toilets: Available in the Trinity Road Stand lower
Contact: (0121) 326 1518 (Bookings are necessary)
E-mail contact: accessibility@avfc.co.uk

Travelling Supporters' Information: From all parts: Exit M6 at Junction 6 (Spaghetti Junction). Follow signs for Birmingham (NE). Take the 4th exit at the roundabout onto the A38 (M) signposted Aston. After ½ mile, turn right into Aston Hall Road.
Bus Services: Service 7 from Colmore Circus to Witton Square. Also some specials.

BRENTFORD FC

Founded: 1889 (**Entered League**: 1920)
Nickname: 'The Bees'
Ground: G tech Community Stadium, 166 Lionel Road North, Brentford TW8 9QT
Ground Capacity: 17,250 (All seats)
Record Attendance: 38,678 (26th February 1949)

Colours: Red & White striped shirts with Black shorts
Telephone Nº: (020) 8847-2511
Ticket Office: 0333 005-8521
Website: www.brentfordfc.com
E-mail: enquiries@brentfordfc.com

GENERAL INFORMATION

Car Parking: Street Parking only. It is recommended that fans do not travel to the Stadium by car but instead use the many nearby public transport links.
Coach Parking: By Police direction
Nearest Railway Station: Kew Bridge (100 metres)
Nearest Tube Station: Gunnersbury (¾ mile)
Bus Routes: Numbers N9,65,237,267 & 391 pass the ground.
Club Shop: At the ground
Opening Times: Weekdays 10.00am–4.00pm and Saturday Matchdays 12.00pm until kick-off and then for one hour after the game.
Telephone Nº: (020) 8847-2511 Option 4

GROUND INFORMATION

Away Supporters' Entrances & Sections:
North east corner

ADMISSION INFO (2024/2025 PRICES)

Adult Seating: £35.00 – £65.00
Senior Citizen Seating: £25.00 – £55.00
Ages 18 to 24 Seating: £25.00 – £55.00
Under-18s Seating: £10.00 – £55.00
Note: Prices vary depending on the category of the game.

FANS WITH DISABILITIES INFORMATION

Wheelchairs: 50 spaces available in total in the West, South and East Stands
Helpers: One helper admitted per fan with disabilities
Prices: Normal prices for fans with disabilities. Helpers free
Disabled Toilets: Available throughout the ground
Contact: (020) 8847-2511 Option 1 (Bookings necessary) accessibility@brentfordfc.com

Travelling Supporters' Information: The stadium is situated just to the south of the M4 and just 100 metres from Kew Bridge station. It is recommended that fans do not travel to the Stadium by car but instead use the many nearby public transport links. In addition to Kew Bridge, the stadium is situated within 1 mile of railway stations at Brentford, Gunnersbury and Kew Gardens and London Underground stations at Acton Town, Gunnersbury and Chiswick Park.

BRIGHTON & HOVE ALBION FC

Founded: 1901 (**Entered League**: 1920)
Nickname: 'Seagulls'
Ground: American Express Community Stadium, Village Way, Brighton   BN1 9BL
Ground Capacity: 30,750 (All seats)
Record Attendance: 30,682 (vs Liverpool, 2019)

Colours: Blue & White striped shirts with Blue shorts
Telephone N°: (01273) 668855
Ticket Office: (01273) 668855 Option 1
Website: www.brightonandhovealbion.com
E-mail: supporter.services@brightonandhovealbion.com

GENERAL INFORMATION

Car Parking: Details of the 2 park & ride sites with a total of 1150 parking spaces can be found on the club website.
Coach Parking: At the stadium
Nearest Railway Station: Falmer (adjacent)
Nearest Bus Station: Brighton
Club Shop: At the stadium
Opening Times: Monday to Saturday 9.30am to 5.00pm and Sundays 11.00am to 4.00pm. Saturday Matchdays open 9.00am to kick-off then after the game until either 6.00pm or 10.30pm, depending on kick-off time.
Telephone N°: (01273) 668855 Option 3

GROUND INFORMATION

Away Supporters' Entrances & Sections:
South Stand

ADMISSION INFO (2024/2025 PRICES)

Adult Seating: £30.00 – £72.00
Under-21s/Senior Citizen Seating: £23.00 – £50.00
Under-18s Seating: £15.00 – £37.00
Note: Prices vary depending on the category of the game.

FANS WITH DISABILITIES INFORMATION

Wheelchairs: 185 spaces available in total
Helpers: One helper admitted per fan with disabilities
Prices: Normal prices for fans with disabilities. Helpers free
Disabled Toilets: Yes – in all the stands
Contact: Find details by clicking on the Disabled Supporters' Booking Guide on the club website.

Travelling Supporters' Information: Routes: From the North: Take the M23 then the A23 to Brighton. At the roundabout on the outskirts of Brighton, take the exit onto the A27 towards Lewes. Pass the A270 turn-off and continue towards the village of Falmer. The stadium is situated by the side of the A27 in the village of Falmer across the road from the University of Sussex campus; From the East and West: Take the A27 to Falmer which is located to the north-east of Brighton. Then as above.

CHELSEA FC

Founded: 1905 (**Entered League**: 1905)
Nickname: 'Blues'
Ground: Stamford Bridge, Fulham Road, London,
SW6 1HS
Ground Capacity: 40,343 (All seats)
Record Attendance: 82,905 (12th October 1935)

Colours: Blue shirts and shorts
Telephone Nº: 0371 811-1955
+44 207 386-9373 (International callers)
Ticket Office: 0371 811-1905
+44 207 835-6000 (International callers)
Website: www.chelseafc.com
E-mail: enquiries@chelseafc.com

GENERAL INFORMATION

Car Parking: Pre-booked underground car park at ground
Coach Parking: By Police direction
Nearest Tube Station: Fulham Broadway (District)
Club Shop: Chelsea Megastore – at the ground
Opening Times: Monday to Saturday 10.00am – 5.00pm;
Sundays 11.00am–5.00pm; Bank Holidays 11.00am – 5.00pm
Closed on home matchdays.
Megastore Telephone Nº: 0371 811 1955

GROUND INFORMATION

Away Supporters' Entrances & Sections:
Shed End

ADMISSION INFO (2024/2025 PRICES)

Adult Seating: £30.00 – £80.00
Child/Senior Citizen Seating: £19.50 – £28.50
Note: Concessionary tickets are available in the Family
Stand, East Upper Stand, Shed Lower and Matthew Harding
Lower stands.

FANS WITH DISABILITIES INFORMATION

Seating: 258 spaces in total (including personal assistants)
for Home and Away fans in the disabled area
Personal Assistants: One admitted per fan with disabilities
Prices: Free of charge for fans with disabilities
Disabled Toilets: Available around the ground
Free commentaries for blind supporters are available
Contact: 0371 811-2012   (Bookings are necessary)

Travelling Supporters' Information:
Routes: From the North & East: Follow Central London signs from the A1/M1 to Hyde Park Corner, then signs for Guildford (A3) to Knightsbridge (A4). After 1 mile turn left into Fulham Road; From the South: Take the A13 or A24 then the A219 to cross Putney Bridge and follow signs for 'West End' (A304) to join the A308 into Fulham Road; From the West: Take the M4 then A4 to Central London, then follow signs to Westminster (A3220). After ¾ mile, turn right at crossroads into Fulham Road.

CRYSTAL PALACE FC

Photo courtesy of Crystal Palace FC

Founded: 1905 (**Entered League**: 1920)
Nickname: 'Eagles'
Ground: Selhurst Park, Whitehorse Lane, London, SE25 6PU
Ground Capacity: 25,486 (All seats)
Record Attendance: 51,482 (11th May 1979)

Colours: Red and Blue striped shirts with Blue shorts
Telephone Nº: (020) 8768-6000
Ticket Office: 0333 360 1861
Website: www.cpfc.co.uk
E-mail: info@cpfc.co.uk

GENERAL INFORMATION

Car Parking: Street Parking only
Coach Parking: Thornton Heath
Nearest Railway Station: Selhurst or Norwood Junction (both 5 minutes walk)
Nearest Bus Station: West Croydon
Club Shop: At the ground
Opening Times: Weekdays & Away Matchdays 9.00am to 5.30pm. Home Matchdays from 9.00am until 30 minutes after kick-off as well as 60 minutes after the final whistle.
Telephone Nº: (020) 8768-6100

GROUND INFORMATION

Away Supporters' Entrances & Sections:
Park Road for the Arthur Wait Stand

ADMISSION INFO (2024/2025 PRICES)

Note: As all 2024/2025 Season Tickets have sold out and matchday seating is very limited please contact the club for details of availability.

FANS WITH DISABILITIES INFORMATION

Wheelchairs: 128 spaces are available around the ground, most of which are on raised viewing platforms
Helpers: One helper admitted per wheelchair
Prices: Concessionary prices apply for fans with disabilities. Helpers are admitted free of charge
Disabled Toilets: Located in the Holmesdale Road Stand
Commentaries are available for 12 people
Contact: (020) 8768-600   dlo@cpfc.co.uk
         (Bookings are necessary)

Travelling Supporters' Information:
Routes: From the North: Take the M1/A1 to the North Circular (A406) for Chiswick. Take the South Circular (A205) to Wandsworth then the A3 to the A214 and follow signs for Streatham to the A23. Turn left onto the B273 after 1 mile, follow to the end, turn left into the High Street and then into Whitehorse Lane; From the East: Take the A232 (Croydon Road) to Shirley and join the A215 (Northwood Road). After 2¼ miles turn left into Whitehorse Lane; From the South: Take the A23 and follow signs for Crystal Palace (B266) through Thornton Heath into Whitehorse Lane; From the West: Take the M4 to Chiswick (then as North).

EVERTON FC

Founded: 1878 (**Entered League**: 1888)
Former Names: St. Domingo's FC (1878-79)
Nickname: 'The Toffees'
Ground: Goodison Park, Goodison Road, Liverpool L4 4EL
Ground Capacity: 39,572 (All seats)
Record Attendance: 78,299 (18th September 1948)

Colours: Blue shirts with White shorts
Telephone N°: (0151) 556-1878
Website: www.evertonfc.com
E-mail: servicedesk@evertonfc.com
Note: A new 52,888-seater stadium is under construction on Bramley-Moore Dock and is expected to be completed during December 2024.

GENERAL INFORMATION
Car Parking: Corner of Priory Road and Utting Avenue
Coach Parking: Priory Road
Nearest Railway Station: Kirkdale
Nearest Mainline Railway Station: Liverpool Lime Street
Nearest Bus Station: Queen's Square, Liverpool
Club Shop: Evertonone Megastore in Walton Lane by the ground plus Evertontwo in Liverpool One Shopping Complex.
Opening Times: Evertonone: Monday to Sunday 10.00am to 4.00pm. Evertontwo: Monday to Saturday 10.00am to 5.00pm and Sundays 11.00am to 5.00pm.
Telephone N°: (0151) 556-1878

GROUND INFORMATION
Away Supporters' Entrances & Sections:
Bullens Road entrances for Bullens Stand – Turnstiles 55-60

ADMISSION INFO (2024/2025 PRICES)
Note: As all 2024/2025 Season Tickets have sold out and matchday seating is very limited please contact the club for details of availability.

FANS WITH DISABILITIES INFORMATION
Wheelchairs: 153 spaces for home fans, 19 spaces for away fans in a special section.
Helpers: One helper admitted per wheelchair
Prices: Normal prices for fans with disabilities. Helpers free.
Disabled Toilets: Available in the section for disabled fans – Radar Key required (available from stewards if necessary). Commentaries are available for the blind
Contact: (0151) 530-5396 or (0151) 319-4033
Brendan Connolly (DAO) – brendan.connolly@evertonfc.com (Bookings are necessary)

Travelling Supporters' Information:
Routes: From the North: Exit the M6 at Junction 26 onto the M58 and continue to it's end. Take the 2nd exit at the roundabout onto the A59 Ormskirk Road. Continue along into Rice Lane and go straight across at the next roundabout into County Road. After ½ mile, turn left into Everton Valley then bear left into Walton Lane for the ground; From the South & East: Exit the M6 at Junction 21A and take the M62 to it's end. Turn right at traffic lights onto A5088 Queen Drive and continue to the junction with Walton Hall Avenue then turn left into Walton Lane (A580) and the ground is on the right.
Bus Services: Services to the ground – 19, 20, F1, F2, 30

FULHAM FC

Founded: 1879 (**Entered League**: 1907)
Former Names: Fulham St. Andrew's FC (1879-1898)
Nickname: 'The Whites'
Ground: Craven Cottage, Stevenage Road, Fulham, London SW6 6HH
Ground Capacity: 24,500 (All seats – when the Riverside development is fully open)

Record Attendance: 49,335 (8th October 1938)
Colours: White shirts with Black shorts
Telephone Nº: 0843 208-1222
Ticket Office: (020) 3871-0810
Website: www.fulhamfc.com
E-mail: enquiries@fulhamfc.com

GENERAL INFORMATION

Car Parking: Street Parking (Matchday restrictions apply)
Coach Parking: Stevenage Road/Fulham Palace Road
Nearest Railway Station: Putney (1 mile)
Nearest Tube Station: Putney Bridge (District) (1 mile)
Club Shop: At the ground and also 959-961 Fulham Road, SW6 5HY
Opening Times: At the ground: Monday to Saturday 9.00am to 5.00pm and Sundays 11.00am to 4.00pm
Telephone Nº: (0203) 871-0815

GROUND INFORMATION

Away Supporters' Entrances & Sections:
Putney End for the Putney Stand

ADMISSION INFO (2024/2025 PRICES)

Adult Seating: £35.00 – £105.00
Concessionary/Under-21s Seating: £30.00 – £80.00
17s and under Seating: £24.00 – £55.00
Note: Prices vary depending on the category of the game and tickets may be cheaper if purchased in advance.

FANS WITH DISABILITIES INFORMATION

Wheelchairs: 68 spaces in total with including 14 spaces for Away fans in the Putney End, Block 7, Gate 1
Helpers: One assistant admitted per fan with disabilities
Prices: Concessionary prices for fans with disabilities. One helper admitted free of charge for each fan in a wheelchair.
Disabled Toilets: Available – access via Radar Key system.
Contact: (020) 3871-0810 (Bookings necessary)

Travelling Supporters' Information:
Routes: From the North: Take the A1/M1 to the North Circular (A406), travel west to Neasden and follow signs for Harlesden A404, then Hammersmith A219. At Broadway, follow the Fulham sign and turn right after 1 mile into Harbord Street then left at the end for the ground; From the South & East: Take the South Circular (A205), follow the Putney Bridge sign (A219). Cross the bridge and follow Hammersmith signs for ½ mile, turn left into Bishops Park Road, then right at the end; From the West: Take the M4 to the A4. Branch left after 2 miles into Hammersmith Broadway (then as from the North).

IPSWICH TOWN FC

Founded: 1878 (**Entered League**: 1938)
Nickname: 'Town' 'Tractor Boys'
Ground: Portman Road, Ipswich IP1 2DA
Ground Capacity: 30,311 (All seats)
Record Attendance: 38,010 (8th March 1975)
Colours: Blue shirts with White shorts

Telephone Nº: (01473) 400500
Ticket Office: 03330 05 05 03
Website: www.itfc.co.uk
E-mail: customer.service@itfc.co.uk

GENERAL INFORMATION

Car Parking: Portman Road and West End Road car parks
Coach Parking: West End Road car park
Nearest Railway Station: Ipswich (5 minutes walk)
Nearest Bus Station: Ipswich
Club Shop: Planet Blue Superstore at the ground
Opening Times: Weekdays 9.00am–5.00pm. Opening times on Matchdays vary. Please contact the club for details
Telephone Nº: (01473) 400501

GROUND INFORMATION

Away Supporters' Entrances & Sections:
Cobbold Stand

ADMISSION INFO (2024/2025 PRICES)

Adult Seating: £26.00 – £58.00
Senior Citizen Seating: £21.00 – £52.00
Under-19s Seating: £9.00 – £44.00
Ages 19 to 23 Seating: £17.00 – £51.00
Under-12s Seating: £6.00 – £7.00

FANS WITH DISABILITIES INFORMATION

Wheelchairs: 103 spaces and 103 seats for home fans in the East of England Cooperative, South and North Stands upper and lower tiers. 10 spaces and 10 seats for away fans in the lower East of England Cooperative Stand only.
Helpers: One helper admitted per fan with disabilities
Prices: Concessionary prices charged for each fan with disabilities plus one helper.
Disabled Toilets: Available around the ground
Commentaries are available for the blind
Contact: (01473) 400556 – lee.smith@itfc.co.uk
(Bookings are necessary)

Travelling Supporters' Information:
Routes: From the North and West: Take the A1214 from the A14/A12 following signs for Ipswich West only. Proceed through Holiday Inn Hotel traffic lights and at the 3rd set of traffic lights turn right into West End Road. The ground is ¼ mile along on the left; From the South: Follow signs for Ipswich West, then as from the North and West above.

LEICESTER CITY FC

Founded: 1884 (**Entered League**: 1894)
Former Names: Leicester Fosse FC (1884-1919)
Nickname: 'Foxes'
Ground: King Power Stadium, Filbert Way, Leicester, LE2 7FL
Ground Capacity: 32,312 (All seats)

Record Attendance: 32,242 (August 2015)
Colours: Blue shirts with White shorts
Telephone N°: 0344 815-5000
Ticket Office: 0344 815-5000 (Option 1)
Website: www.lcfc.com
E-mail: lcfchelp@lcfc.co.uk

GENERAL INFORMATION

Car Parking: NCP Car Park (5 minutes walk). Some pre-booked spaces at the ground may be available (£17.00) and a Park and Ride service is available from Enderby
Coach Parking: Sawday Street
Nearest Railway Station: Leicester (1 mile)
Nearest Bus Station: St. Margaret's (1 mile)
Club Shop: At the ground
Opening Times: Monday to Saturday 9.00am to 6.00pm. Saturday Matchdays open 9.00am until kick-off then for 30 minutes after the game. Sundays open 10.00am – 4.00pm
Telephone N°: 0344 815-5000 Option 7

GROUND INFORMATION

Away Supporters' Entrances & Sections:
At the corner of the North and East Stands – Turnstiles 40-49

ADMISSION INFO (2024/2025 PRICES)

Adult Seating: £33.00 – £72.00
Senior Citizen Seating: £31.00 – £59.00
Under-22s Seating: £31.00 – £59.00
Under-18s Seating: £25.00 – £46.00
Under-16s Seating: £17.00 – £35.00
Under-12s Seating: £8.00 – £22.00
Note: Prices vary depending on the category of the game.

FANS WITH DISABILITIES INFORMATION

Wheelchairs: 186 spaces for wheelchairs plus 111 spaces for helpers accommodated at various levels in all stands
Helpers: One carer admitted per fan with disabilities
Prices: Reduced prices are available – Phone for details
Disabled Toilets: Available in all stands
Contact: 0344 815-5000 Option 4 – disability@lcfc.co.uk

Travelling Supporters' Information:
Routes: From the North: Take the A46/A607 into the City Centre or exit the M1 at Junction 21, take the A5460, turn right ¾ mile after the Railway Bridge into Upperton Road, then right into Filbert Way; From the East: Take the A47 into the City Centre (then as from the North); From the South: Exit the M1 at Junction 21 and take the A5460, turn right ¾ mile after Railway Bridge into Upperton Road, then right into Filbert Way; From the West: Take the M69 to the City Centre (then as from North).

LIVERPOOL FC

Founded: 1892 (**Entered League**: 1893)
Nickname: 'Reds'
Ground: Anfield Road, Liverpool   L4 0TH
Ground Capacity: 61,000 (including rail seats)
Record Attendance: 61,905 (2nd February 1952)

Colours: Red shirts, shorts and socks
Telephone Nº: (0151) 264-2500
Website: www.liverpoolfc.com
E-mail: via link on website

GENERAL INFORMATION

Car Parking: None available in the immediate area
Coach Parking: Priory Road and Pinehurst Avenue
Nearest Railway Station: Kirkdale (¾ mile)
Nearest Bus Station: Paradise Street, Liverpool
Club Shop: At the ground, at Williamson Square and 'Liverpool One' in the City Centre, at 48 Eastgate Street, Chester CH1 1LE , at 9 Castle Lane, Belfast   BT1 5DA
Opening Times: At Anfield: Monday to Saturday 9.00am to 5.30pm and Sunday 10.00am to 4.00pm; Chester: Monday to Saturday 9.00am to 5.00pm (until 6pm Thursday to Saturday) and Sunday 11.00am to 5.00pm; At Liverpool One: Monday to Saturday 9.30am to 7.00pm and Sunday 11.00am – 5.00pm; At Williamson Square: Monday to Saturday 9.00am to 6.30pm and Sunday 10.00am – 4.00pm; At Belfast: Monday to Saturday 9.30am to 5.30pm and Sunday 1.00pm to 5.00pm.
Telephone Nº: (0151) 264-2368 (Anfield store)

GROUND INFORMATION

Away Supporters' Entrances & Sections:
Anfield Road

ADMISSION INFO (2024/2025 PRICES)

Adult Seating: £30.00 – £61.00
Senior Citizen Seating: £29.25 – £45.75
Young Adult Seating: £19.50 – £30.50
Junior Seating: £9.00

FANS WITH DISABILITIES INFORMATION

Wheelchairs: 239 spaces in total around the ground including 24 spaces for away fans in the Anfield Road Stand.
Helpers: One helper is admitted per wheelchair but a second helper can sometimes be accommodated
Prices: £14.63 to £45.75 for fans with disabilities, dependent on age. One helper is admitted free of charge with each fan with disabilities.
Disabled Toilets: Two available in the Paddock, two in the Kop Stand and one in the Anfield Road Stand
Commentaries are available for the visually impaired on request
Contact: By email - disability@liverpoolfc.com

Travelling Supporters' Information:
Routes: From the North: Exit the M6 at Junction 28 and follow Liverpool A580 signs into Walton Hall Avenue, pass Stanley Park and turn left into Anfield Road; From the South and East: Take the M62 to the end of the motorway, then turn right into Queen's Drive (A5058) and turn left after 3 miles into Utting Avenue. After 1 mile, turn right into Anfield Road; From North Wales: Take the Mersey Tunnel into the City Centre and follow signs for Preston (A580) into Walton Hall Avenue. Turn right into Anfield Road before Stanley Park.

MANCHESTER CITY FC

Founded: 1887 (**Entered League**: 1892)
Former Name: St.Mark's FC, Ardwick FC (1887-1894)
Nickname: 'Cityzens' 'City' 'Blues'
Ground: Etihad Stadium, Etihad Campus, Manchester M11 3FF
Record Attendance: 54,693 (February 2016)

Ground Capacity: 55,097 (All seats) (To increase to over 60,000 following redevelopment)
Colours: Sky Blue shirtswith White shorts
Telephone Nº: (0161) 444-1894 Option 5
Website: www.mancity.com
E-mail: mancity@mancity.com

GENERAL INFORMATION

Car Parking: 1,000 spaces available at the stadium. Another 7,000 spaces are available off site in the vicinity.
Coach Parking: Around 40 spaces available at the stadium
Nearest Railway Station: Ashburys (15 minutes walk) or Manchester Piccadilly (20 minutes walk)
Nearest Bus Station: 53,54,185,186,216,217,230,231,232, 233,234,235,236,237,X36 & X37 services stop at the stadium
Club Shop: At the stadium
Opening Times: Monday to Saturday 9.00am to 5.30pm, Sundays 11.00am to 5.00pm and before and after matches.
Telephone Nº: (0161) 444-1894 Option 3

GROUND INFORMATION

Away Supporters' Entrances & Sections:
South Stand

ADMISSION INFO (2024/2025 PRICES)

As most 2024/2025 fixtures are already sold out please contact the club for further information.

FANS WITH DISABILITIES INFORMATION

Wheelchairs: 255 spaces available in total including 21 for away fans
Helpers: One helper admitted per disabled fan
Prices: Concessionary prices for the disabled. Helpers free
Disabled Toilets: 42 wheelchair accessible toilets are available around the stadium
Commentaries for the blind and lifts are also available
Contact: (0161) 438-7834 (Bookings are recommended)

Travelling Supporters' Information:
Routes: From the North: Exit the M60 at Junction 23 onto the A635 then turn right onto the A662 Ashton New Road. The stadium is approximately 1½ miles on the right hand side; From the East: Exit the M60 at Junction 24 and follow the A57 into Manchester before turning right onto the A6010 for the stadium; From the South: Follow the A6 into Manchester and then turn right onto the A6010 for the stadium. Alternatively, exit the M60 at Junction 1 and follow the A34 Kingsway into Manchester before turning right onto the A6010 for the stadium; From the West: Take the M602 into Manchester and continue onto the A57 then the A57(M) Mancunian Way onto the A635. Follow the road right before turning left onto the A6010 for the stadium.

MANCHESTER UNITED FC

Founded: 1878 (**Entered League**: 1892)	**Record Attendance**: 76,962 (25th March 1939)
Former Names: Newton Heath LYR FC (1878-1892), Newton Heath FC (1892-1902)	**Colours**: Red shirts with White shorts
Nickname: 'Red Devils'	**Telephone N°**: (0161) 868-8000 Option 4
Ground: Sir Matt Busby Way, Old Trafford, Manchester M16 0RA	**Ticket Information**: (0161) 868-8000 Option 1
Ground Capacity: 74,994 (All seats)	**Website**: www.manutd.com
	E-mail: enquiries@manutd.co.uk

GENERAL INFORMATION

Car Parking: Lancashire Cricket Ground and Car Park E3 on John Gilbert Way. Other approved car parks are signposted

Coach Parking: By Police direction

Nearest Railway Station: At the ground

Nearest Bus Station: Chorlton Street

Nearest Metro Station: Old Trafford (located at L.C.C.C.) and also Salford Quays

Club Shop: At the ground

Opening Times: Non-matchdays: Monday to Saturday 10.00am – 5.00pm and Sundays 11.00am to 5.00pm. Saturday Matchdays 9.00am to 5.30pm for early kick-offs, 9.30am to 6.00pm (3pm kick-off), 9.30am to 8.30pm (5.30pm kick-off) and 9.30am to 10.45pm (8.00pm kick-off). Sundays 10.30am – 4.30pm (1.30pm kick-off) and 10.00am to 4.00pm (4.00pm kick-off).

Magastore Telephone N°: (0161) 868-8567

Museum & Tour Centre: (0161) 868-8000 (Option 3)

GROUND INFORMATION

Away Supporters' Entrances & Sections: Bobby Charlton (South) Stand (turnstile 22) and East Stand (turnstile 30)

ADMISSION INFO (2024/2025 PRICES)

As most 2024/2025 fixtures are already sold out please contact the club for further information.

FANS WITH DISABILITIES INFORMATION

Wheelchairs: 160 spaces in total for Home and Away fans in sections in the North East & North West quadrants

Helpers: One helper admitted per fan with disabilities

Prices: Concessionary prices charge for fans with disabilities. Helpers are admitted free of charge

Disabled Toilets: Available

Commentaries are available for the visually impaired

Contact: (0161) 868-8009 (Bookings are necessary)

E-mail: accessibility@manutd.co.uk

Travelling Supporters' Information:

Routes: From the North and West: Take the M61 to the M60 and exit at Junction 4 following Manchester (A5081) signs. Turn right after 2½ miles into Sir Matt Busby Way for the ground; From the South: Exit the M6 at Junction 19 and take Stockport (A556) road then Altrincham (A56). From Altrincham follow Manchester signs and turn left into Sir Matt Busby Way after 6 miles; From the East: Exit the M62 at Junction 17 and take the A56 to Manchester. Follow signs for the South then signs for Chester (Chester Road). Turn right into Sir Matt Busby Way after 2 miles.

NEWCASTLE UNITED FC

Founded: 1882 (**Entered League**: 1893)
Former Names: Newcastle East End FC (1882-1892)
amalgamated with Newcastle West End FC
Nickname: 'Magpies'
Ground: St. James Park, Strawberry Place,
Newcastle-Upon-Tyne NE1 4ST
Ground Capacity: 52,354 (All seats)

Record Attendance: 68,386 (3rd September 1930)
Colours: Black and White striped shirts, Black shorts
Telephone Nº: 0344 372-1892
Ticket Office: 0344 372-1892
Website: www.nufc.co.uk
E-mail: boxoffice@nufc.co.uk

GENERAL INFORMATION
Car Parking: Street parking
Coach Parking: By Police direction
Nearest Railway Station: Newcastle Central (¼ mile)
Nearest Bus Station: St. James' Boulevard (¼ mile)
Club Shop: At the ground
Opening Times: Monday to Saturday 9.00am – 5.00pm
Telephone Nº: 0344 372-1892

GROUND INFORMATION
Away Supporters' Entrances & Sections:
Rear of the Leazes Stand, entrance from Barrack Road
through turnstiles 91-94

ADMISSION INFO (2024/2025 PRICES)
As most 2024/2025 fixtures are already sold out please
contact the club for further information.

FANS WITH DISABILITIES INFORMATION
Wheelchairs: 160 spaces in total in special areas
throughout the stadium Lifts are available.
Helpers: One helper admitted per fan with disabilities
Prices: Half-price tickets for fans with disabilities. Helpers
are admitted free of charge
Disabled Toilets: Throughout the stadium (via Radar Key)
Commentaries are available for 20 blind supporters
Contact: (0191) 201-8457 or disability.support@nufc.co.uk

Travelling Supporters' Information:
Routes: From the North: Follow the A1 into Newcastle, then follow Hexham signs into Percy Street. Turn right into Leazes Park
Road; From the South: Take the A1M, then after Birtley Granada Services take the A1 Gateshead Western Bypass (bear left on
the Motorway). Follow Airport signs for approximately 3 miles then take the A692 (Newcastle) sign, crossing the Redheugh
Bridge. Proceed over three sets of traffic lights to the roundabout and take the 1st exit into Barrack Road; From the West: Take
the A69 towards the City Centre. Pass Newcastle General Hospital. At the traffic lights after the Hospital turn left into Brighton
Grove. After 70 yards turn right into Stanhope Street and proceed into Barrack Road for the ground.

NOTTINGHAM FOREST FC

Founded: 1865 (**Entered League**: 1892)
Nickname: 'The Reds'
Ground: The City Ground, Pavilion Road,
Nottingham   NG2 5FJ
Ground Capacity: 30,445 (All seats)

Record Attendance: 49,946 (28th October 1967)
Colours: Red shirts with White shorts
Telephone Nº: (0115) 982-4444
Website: www.nottinghamforest.co.uk
E-mail: reception@nottinghamforest.co.uk

GENERAL INFORMATION

Car Parking: Various nearby car parks and street parking
Coach Parking: Available at the stadium.
Nearest Railway Station: Nottingham Midland (½ mile)
Nearest Bus Station: Victoria Street/Broadmarsh Centre
Club Shop: At the ground
Opening Times: Weekdays 9.00am – 5.00pm; Matchdays 9.00am – kick-off and 30 minutes after the game; Sunday matchdays 10.00am – kick-off + 60 minutes after the game
Telephone Nº: (0115) 982-4305

GROUND INFORMATION

Away Supporters' Entrances & Sections:
Entrances via East car park for Bridgford Stand

ADMISSION INFO (2024/2025 PRICES)

Adult Seating: £38.00 – £49.00
Concessionary Seating: £32.00 – £39.00
Ages 12 to 19 Seating: £19.00 – £29.00
Under-12s Seating: £12.00 – £15.00

FANS WITH DISABILITIES INFORMATION

Wheelchairs: 68 spaces in total for home fans around the ground plus 11 spaces for away fans in the Lower Bridgford Stand
Helpers: One helper admitted per fan with disabilities
Prices: Please contact the club for further information
Disabled Toilets: 7 available with radar key locks
Contact: Disability Liaison Officer - Eamon Collins

Travelling Supporters' Information:
Routes: From the North: Exit the M1 at Junction 26 following Nottingham signs (A610) then signs to Melton Mowbray and Trent Bridge (A606). Cross the River Trent, turn left into Radcliffe Road then left again into Colwick Road for the ground; From the South: Exit the M1 at Junction 24 following signs for Nottingham (South) to Trent Bridge. Turn right into Radcliffe Road then left into Colwick Road; From the East: Take the A52 to West Bridgford and follow signs for Football & Cricket; From the West: Take the A52 into Nottingham, follow signs for Melton Mowbray and Trent Bridge, cross the River Trent (then as North).

SOUTHAMPTON FC

Founded: 1885 (**Entered League**: 1920)
Former Names: Southampton St. Mary's YMCA FC (1885-1897)
Nickname: 'Saints'
Ground: St. Mary's Stadium, Britannia Road, Southampton   SO14 5FP
Ground Capacity: 32,384 (All seats)

Record Attendance: 32,363 (28th April 2012)
Colours: Red and White shirts with Black shorts
Telephone Nº: 02380 727700
Ticket Office: 02381 780780
Website: www.southamptonfc.com
E-mail: reception@saintsfc.co.uk

GENERAL INFORMATION

Car Parking: Park & Ride must be pre-booked or Marina area car parks (£5.00)
Coach Parking: By Police direction
Nearest Railway Station: Southampton Central
Nearest Bus Station: Western Esplanade – services 7, 16, 18, X4 and X5 all travel to the stadium
Club Shop: At the ground and also at West Quay
Opening Times: Monday to Friday 9.00am to 5.00pm and Saturdays 9.30am to 5.00pm
Telephone Nº: 02380 711973 (Stadium)
02380 337104 (West Quay)

GROUND INFORMATION

Away Supporters' Entrances & Sections:
Northam Stand – Blocks 43 to 48

ADMISSION INFO (2024/2025 PRICES)

Note: Please contact the club for this information for the 2024-2025 season.

FANS WITH DISABILITIES INFORMATION

Wheelchairs: 193 spaces in total for Home and Away fans throughout the ground
Helpers: One helper admitted per fan with disabilities
Prices: Concessionary prices are charged
Disabled Toilets: Available in all Stands – Radar key required
Contact: 02380 711980   (Bookings are necessary)
E-mail Contact: supporterrelations@saintsfc.co.uk

Travelling Supporters' Information:
Routes: Although the ground is situated in the Melbourne Street/Marine Parade area of Southampton, no parking is available in the immediate vicinity except by special arrangement for Disabled supporters. There are a number of well-signposted Park and Ride car parks around the City and those designated for Away fans should be clearly marked.

TOTTENHAM HOTSPUR FC

Founded: 1882 (**Entered League**: 1908)
Former Name: Hotspur FC (1882-1884)
Nickname: 'Spurs'
Ground: Tottenham Hotspur Stadium,
White Hart Lane, Bill Nicholson Way, 782 High Road,
Tottenham, London   N17 0BX
Ground Capacity: 62,062 (All seats)

Record Attendance: 61,104 (vs Chelsea, 22/12/19)
Colours: White shirts with Navy Blue shorts
Telephone Nº: 0344 499-5000
Ticket Office: 0344 844-0102
Website: www.tottenhamhotspur.com
E-mail: supporter.services@tottenhamhotspur.com

GENERAL INFORMATION

Car Parking: None within ¼ mile of the ground
Coach Parking: Northumberland Park, West Road – Parking permit required
Nearest Railway Station: White Hart Lane (nearby) or Northumberland Park
Nearest Tube Station: Seven Sisters (Victoria Line) or Manor House (Piccadilly Line)
Club Shop: At the stadium and in Chelmsford, Harlow and Stevenage
Opening Times: Stadium store: Monday to Saturday 9.30am – 5.30pm and Sunday 10.00am – 4.00pm. The stores in Chelmsford, Harlow and Stevenage close at 4.30pm from Monday to Saturday.
Telephone Nº: 0344 499-5000 or (020) 8365-5042

GROUND INFORMATION

Away Supporters' Entrances & Sections:
North east corner of the stadium – Blocks 114-118 & 234

ADMISSION INFO (2024/2025 PRICES)

As most 2024/2025 fixtures are already sold out please contact the club for further information.

FANS WITH DISABILITIES INFORMATION

Wheelchairs: 265 spaces available in total around the stadium. Away fans in wheelchairs please use entrance 11a.
Helpers: Admitted
Prices: Normal prices for disabled fans. Helpers free of charge
Disabled Toilets: 66 available throughout the stadium
Contact: (020) 8365-5360   (Bookings are necessary)

Travelling Supporters' Information:
Routes: From All Parts: Take the A406 North Circular to Edmonton and at traffic lights follow signs for Tottenham (A1010) into Fore Street for the ground.

WEST HAM UNITED FC

Photograph courtesy of Queen Elizabeth Olympic Park

Founded: 1895 (**Entered League**: 1919)
Former Name: Thames Ironworks FC
Nickname: 'Hammers'
Ground: London Stadium, Queen Elizabeth Olympic Park, Marsh Gate Lane, London E20 2ST
Ground Capacity: 62,500 (All seats)

Record Attendance: 59,988 (vs Everton 30/3/2019)
Colours: Claret and Blue shirts with White shorts
Telephone N°: (020) 8548-2748
Ticket Office: 03330 301966
Website: www.whufc.com
E-mail: supporterservices@westhamunited.co.uk

GENERAL INFORMATION

Car Parking: Limited spaces available at the Olympic Park. See Travelling Supporters' Information below for more details
Nearest Railway Station: Stratford (20 minutes walk)
Nearest Tube Station: Stratford (20 minutes walk)
Club Shops: At the Stadium and also at Lakeside Thurrock, Liberty Romford and Basildon
Opening Times: Vary by store. Stadium opening hours are Monday to Saturday 9.30am to 5.00pm (from 9.00am on Saturdays) and Sunday 11.00am to 5.00pm.
Telephone N°: (01708) 890258 (Lakeside Store) or (01708) 741877 (Liberty Romford)

GROUND INFORMATION

Away Supporters' Entrances & Sections:
South West corner of the stadium – Block D

ADMISSION INFO (2024/2025 PRICES)

Adult Seating: £45.00 – £105.00
Senior Citizen Seating: £45.00 – £105.00
Under-21s Seating: £45.00 – £105.00
Under-16s Seating: £45.00 – £105.00
Note: Prices above are for the highest category matches.

FANS WITH DISABILITIES INFORMATION

Wheelchairs: 253 spaces available throughout the stadium inncluding 24 for away fans
Helpers: Admitted
Prices: Concessionary prices apply for fans with disabilities. Free of charge for helpers
Disabled Toilets: 49 available in all areas of the stadium
Contact: 03330 300174 (Bookings are necessary) or accessibility@westhamunited.co.uk

Travelling Supporters' Information:
Routes: Due to the fact that there is restricted car parking in the area of the stadium, it is recommended that visitors use the many public transport links available nearby, with tube and rail links plus numerous bus and coach routes close to the stadium. For those who choose to travel by car, the stadium is located in the Stratford area of east London, just to the east of the A12 and to the north of the River Thames. Visitors travelling by car are advised to use the public car parks at the Westfield Stratford City shopping centre, Stratford International station and the Stratford Centre.

WOLVERHAMPTON WANDERERS FC

Founded: 1877 (**Entered League**: 1888)
Former Names: Formed by the amalgamation of St. Luke's FC and The Wanderers Football & Cricket Club in 1879. St. Luke's is considered the start of the club
Nickname: 'Wolves'
Ground: Molineux Stadium, Waterloo Road, Wolverhampton WV1 4QR
Ground Capacity: 31,700 (All seats)

Record Attendance: 61,305 (11th February 1939)
Colours: Gold shirts with Black shorts
Telephone Nº: (01902) 810485
Ticket Office: 0371 222-1877
Website: www.wolves.co.uk
E-mail: fanservices@wolves.co.uk

GENERAL INFORMATION

Car Parking: Around West Park, Newhampton Road and rear of the Stan Cullis Stand. Also in City Centre (5 minutes walk)
Coach Parking: By Police direction
Nearest Railway Station: Wolverhampton (¾ mile)
Nearest Bus Station: Wolverhampton (¾ mile)
Club Shop: At the ground
Opening Times: Daily from 9.00am to 5.00pm
Telephone Nº: (01902) 810485

GROUND INFORMATION

Away Supporters' Entrances & Sections:
Steve Bull Stand Lower Tier (turnstiles for Block 3)

ADMISSION INFO (2024/2025 PRICES)

As most 2024/2025 fixtures are already sold out please contact the club for further information.

FANS WITH DISABILITIES INFORMATION

Wheelchairs: 115 spaces for home fans in the Stan Cullis Stand and Billy Wright Family Enclosure plus 14 spaces for away fans in the Steve Bull Lower Stand
Helpers: Admitted
Prices: Please contact the club for details
Disabled Toilets: At both ends of the Stan Cullis Stand
Contact: (01902) 810485

Travelling Supporters' Information:
Routes: From North: Exit M6 Junction 12. At island take 3rd exit onto A5 for Wolverhampton. At next island turn left onto A449. After 6 miles A449 passes under M54, carry straight on and at 6th roundabout (Five Ways) take 3rd exit into Waterloo Road. Molineux is 1 mile straight on; From South West: Exit M5 Junction 2, follow signs for Wolverhampton on A4123 for 8 miles to ring road. Turn left on ring road (follow Molineux Centre signs). Take 2nd exit at next 2 islands * Pass Bank's Brewery and Swimming Baths on left and turn left at next set of traffic lights. Molineux is 500 yards on right; From South/East: Exit M6 Junction 10, take A454 (via Willenhall) to Wolverhampton ring road. At first ring road island take 4th exit (A449 to Stafford). Straight on at next 2 sets of traffic lights. Filter right at third set of lights (Waterloo Road). Molineux is 500 yards on right; From West: Take A41 to Wolverhampton ring road roundabout. Turn left into the ring road. Then as from the South West *

EFL CHAMPIONSHIP

Website   www.efl.com
Email   info@efltrust.com

<u>Clubs for the 2024/2025 Season</u>

BLACKBURN ROVERS FC

Founded: 1875 (**Entered League**: 1888)
Nickname: 'Rovers' 'Blues & Whites'
Ground: Ewood Park, Blackburn   BB2 4JF
Ground Capacity: 31,367 (All seats)
Record Attendance: 62,255 vs Bolton (2/3/1929)

Colours: Blue and White halved shirts, White shorts
Telephone Nº: (01254) 372001
Ticket Office: (01254) 372000
Website: www.rovers.co.uk
Contact E-mail: enquiries@rovers.co.uk

GENERAL INFORMATION

Car Parking: 800 spaces available at the ground
Coach Parking: At the ground (Darwen End)
Nearest Railway Station: Blackburn Central (1½ miles)
Nearest Bus Station: Blackburn Central (1½ miles)
Club Shop: Roverstore at the ground
Opening Times: Weekdays 9.00am – 5.00pm, Saturday 10.00am–3.00pm, closed on Sundays.
Telephone Nº: (01254) 508137 (Ewood shop)

GROUND INFORMATION

Away Supporters' Entrances & Sections:
Darwen End

ADMISSION INFO (2024/2025 PRICES)

Adult Seating: £25.00
Senior Citizen Seating: £20.00
Ages 18 to 23 Seating: £15.00
Student Seating: £10.00
Under-18s Seating: £7.00

FANS WITH DISABILITIES INFORMATION

Wheelchairs: 262 spaces for Home fans and 30 for Away fans
Helpers: One helper admitted per fan with disabilities. Applications for helpers tickets must be made in advance
Prices: Normal prices apply for both fans with disabilities and their helpers
Disabled Toilets: 14 purpose-built ground level toilets
Commentaries available via Radio Rovers – bring a radio!
Contact: 0771 772-4646   **E-mail**: chaines@rovers.co.uk
Christina Haines – (01254) 508226

Travelling Supporters' Information: Routes: Supporters travelling Northbound on the M6: Exit the M6 at Junction 29, follow the M65 and exit at Junction 4 for Ewood Park. The ground is ¾ mile from Junction 4 – please look for parking areas to avoid congestion around the ground; Supporters travelling Northbound on the M61: Exit the M61 at Junction 9, join the M65 and exit at Junction 4 (then as above); Supporters travelling Southbound on the M6: Exit the M6 at Junction 30, follow the M61 and exit at Junction 9 onto the M65. Exit the M65 at Junction 4 for the ground; Supporters from the Yorkshire Area either on the B6234, the A56 Haslingden by-pass or the A59 Skipton Road – please follow signs for Ewood Park (follow Preston M65 and exit at Junction 4).

BRISTOL CITY FC

Founded: 1894 (**Entered League**: 1901)
Former Name: Bristol South End FC (1894-1897)
Nickname: 'The Robins'
Ground: Ashton Gate Stadium, Bristol BS3 2EJ
Ground Capacity: 27,000 (All seats)
Record Attendance: 43,335 (16th February 1935)

Colours: Red shirts with White shorts
Telephone Nº: (0117) 963-0600
Ticket Hotline: (0117) 963-0600 (Option 1)
Website: www.bcfc.co.uk
E-mail: supporterservices@bristol-sport.co.uk

GENERAL INFORMATION

Car Parking: Street parking and also at Bedminster Cricket Club (5 minutes walk)
Coach Parking: By prior arrangement with the club
Nearest Railway Station: Bristol Temple Meads (1½ miles)
Nearest Bus Station: Bristol City Centre
Club Shop: BCFC Megastore at the ground
Opening Times: Monday to Saturday 9.00am to 5.00pm and weekend matchdays from 5.00pm until half an hour after the final whistle.
Telephone Nº: (0117) 963-0600 (Option 0 then Option 1)

GROUND INFORMATION

Away Supporters' Entrances & Sections:
Atyeo Stand – Turnstiles 39-46 via Ashton Road

ADMISSION INFO (2024/2025 PRICES)

Adult Seating: £30.00 – £47.00
Under-25s/Senior Citizen Seating: £26.00 – £44.00
Under-22s Seating: £24.00 – £40.00
Under-19s Seating: £18.00 – £26.00
Under-12s Seating: £12.00 – £21.00
Note: A membership scheme offers discounted prices for advance bookings.

FANS WITH DISABILITIES INFORMATION

Wheelchairs: 159 spaces are available (20 for away fans)
Helpers: One helper admitted per fan with disabilities
Prices: Normal prices for fans with disabilities. Helpers free
Disabled Toilets: Available in various areas of the ground
Commentaries are available for the blind
Contact: (0117) 963-0600 Option 1 (Bookings are necessary)
supporterservices@bristol-sport.co.uk

Travelling Supporters' Information: Routes: From the North & West: Exit the M5 at Junction 16, take the A38 to Bristol City Centre and follow the A38 Taunton signs. Cross the swing bridge after 1¼ miles and bear left into Winterstoke Road for the ground; From the East: Take the M4 then M32 and follow signs for the City Centre. Then as for North and West; From the South: Exit the M5 at Junction 19 and follow Taunton signs over the swing bridge (then as above).
Away Fans Car Parking: Bedminster Cricket Club, Clanidge Road, Bristol – SatNav: BS3 2JX (½ mile from Ashton Gate)
Bus Services: Services 27A and 28A from Bristol Temple Meads Station. A bus leaves Temple Meads 1 hour prior to kick-off.

BURNLEY FC

Founded: 1882 (**Entered League**: 1888)
Former Name: Burnley Rovers FC
Nickname: 'Clarets'
Ground: Turf Moor, Harry Potts Way, Burnley,
Lancashire BB10 4BX
Ground Capacity: 21,944 (All seats)
Record Attendance: 54,775 (23rd February 1924)

Colours: Claret and Sky Blue shirts and shorts
Telephone Nº: (01282) 446800
Ticket Office: (01282) 446800 Option 1
Website: www.burnleyfootballclub.com
E-mail: info@burnleyfc.com

GENERAL INFORMATION

Car Parking: Matchday parking restrictions in surrounding streets so it is recommended that the various Town Centre car parks are used by visiting fans.
Coach Parking: By Police direction
Nearest Railway Station: Burnley Central (1½ miles)
Nearest Bus Station: Burnley (5 minutes walk)
Club Shop: At the ground and at Charter Walk Shopping Centre, 4 Fleet Walk, Burnley BB11 1QE
Opening Times: At Turf Moor: Monday to Friday and non-match Saturdays 10.00am – 4.00pm; Saturday matchdays open from 10.00am to kick-off then for 1 hour after the game. At Charter Walk: Monday to Saturday 9.00am to 5.30pm and Sunday 10.00am – 4.00pm.
Telephone Nº: (01282) 700016 or (01282) 453914

GROUND INFORMATION

Away Supporters' Entrances & Sections:
Ladbrokes Stand

ADMISSION INFO (2024/2025 PRICES)

Please contact the club for matchday admission prices as details were unavailable when we went to print.

FANS WITH DISABILITIES INFORMATION

Wheelchairs: 42 spaces available in the four designated wheelchair areas arounnd the ground.
Helpers: One helper admitted for each wheelchair user
Prices: Normal prices apply for fans with disabilities plus one helper admitted free of charge
Disabled Toilets: Available
Commentary radios are available to purchase for a nominal fee.
Contact: (01282) 704704 (Bookings are necessary) –
slo@burnleyfc.com

Travelling Supporters' Information: Routes: From the North: Follow the A682 to the Town Centre and take first exit at roundabout (Gala Club) into Yorkshire Street. Follow through traffic signals into Harry Potts Way; From the East: Follow the A646 to the A671 then along Todmorden Road towards the Town Centre. At the traffic signals (crossroads) turn right into Harry Potts Way; From the West & South: Exit the M6 at Junction 29 onto the M65. Exit the M65 at Junction 10 and follow signs for Burnley Football Club. At the roundabout in the town centre take the third exit into Yorkshire Street. Then as from the North.

CARDIFF CITY FC

Founded: 1899 (**Entered League**: 1920)
Former Names: Riverside FC (1899-1902) and Riverside Albion FC (1902-1908)
Nickname: 'Bluebirds'
Ground: Cardiff City Stadium, Leckwith Road, Cardiff CF11 8AZ
Record Attendance: 33,028 (22nd December 2018)

Ground Capacity: 33,316 (All seats)
Colours: Blue shirts and shorts
Telephone Nº: 0333 311-1927
Ticket Office: 0333 311-1920
Website: www.cardiffcityfc.co.uk
E-mail: club@cardiffcityfc.co.uk

GENERAL INFORMATION

Car Parking: Stadium car park and Street Parking
Coach Parking: Stadium car park (adjacent)
Nearest Railway Station: Cardiff Central (1 mile) and also Ninian Park Station (500 yards)
Nearest Bus Station: Cardiff Central
Club Shop: At the ground
Opening Times: Weekdays from 9.00am to 5.00pm and Saturdays 10.00am to 4.00pm
Telephone Nº: 0333 311-1922
Postal Sales: Yes (Internet Sales also accepted)

GROUND INFORMATION

Away Supporters' Entrances & Sections:
Grange End, Gate 07 – sections 119 to 122

ADMISSION INFO (2024/2025 PRICES)

Adult Seating: £22.00 – £40.00
Concessionary Seating: £19.00 – £33.00
Ages 16 to 21 Seating: £15.00 – £29.00
Under-16s Seating: £11.00 – £22.00
Note: Prices vary depending on the classification of the game and cheaper prices are available in the Family area.

FANS WITH DISABILITIES INFORMATION

Wheelchairs: Numerous spaces available for fans with disabilities in various areas around the ground
Helpers: One helper admitted per fan with disabilities
Prices: Normal prices for fans with disabilities. Helpers admitted free of charge
Disabled Toilets: Available – access via Radar Key system
Contact: 0333 311-1927 (Away fans tickets are normally sold in advance but may be available on the day) – ben.jones@cardiffcityfc.co.uk

Travelling Supporters' Information:
Routes: From All Parts: Exit M4 at Junction 33 and follow Penarth (A4232) signs. After 6 miles, take the B4267 to Cardiff City Stadium.

COVENTRY CITY FC

Founded: 1883 (**Entered League**: 1919)
Former Names: Singers FC (1883-1898)
Nickname: 'Sky Blues'
Ground: Coventry Building Society Arena, Dodds Lane, Foleshill, Coventry CV6 6GE
Ground Capacity: 32,400 (All seats)
Record Attendance: 51,455 (At Highfield Road)

Colours: Sky Blue shirts and socks, White shorts
Telephone N°: (024) 7699-1987
Website: www.ccfc.co.uk
E-mail: info@ccfc.co.uk
Postal Address: Sky Blue Lodge, Leamington Road, Ryton-on-Dunsmore, Coventry CV8 3FL

GENERAL INFORMATION

Car Parking: 2,000 spaces available at the ground. Please pre-book parking via www.ricoharena.com or the ticket office
Coach Parking: At the ground (Car Park 'C')
Nearest Railway Station: Coventry (3 miles)
Nearest Bus Station: Coventry (3 miles)
Club Shop: At the ground and in the City Centre
Opening Times: Weekday office hours and Matchdays
Telephone N°: (024) 7767-2021

GROUND INFORMATION

Away Supporters' Entrances & Sections:
Turnstiles 1-11 for South Stand accommodation

ADMISSION INFO (2024/2025 PRICES)

Adult Seating: £24.00 – £37.00
Concessionary Seating: £19.00 – £32.00
Under-18s Seating: £15.00 – £25.00
Under-14s Seating: £10.00 – £15.00
Note: Tickets are cheaper when purchased in advance

FANS WITH DISABILITIES INFORMATION

Wheelchairs: 94 spaces available in total
Helpers: Admitted
Prices: Normal prices apply for fans with disabilities. Free of charge for helpers
Disabled Toilets: Available
Contact: (024) 7699-2335   jodie.jones@ccfc.co.uk
(Bookings are necessary)

Travelling Supporters' Information:
Routes: From All Parts: Exit the M6 at Junction 3 and follow the A444 towards Coventry. The ground is located just 400 yards along this road. Please note that parking spaces at the ground must be pre-booked. No street parking.

DERBY COUNTY FC

Founded: 1884 (**Entered League**: 1888)
Nickname: 'Rams'
Ground: Pride Park Stadium, Royal Way,
Pride Park, Derby   DE24 8XL
Ground Capacity: 33,597 (All seats)
Record Attendance: 33,475 (1st May 2006)

Colours: White shirts with Black shorts
Telephone Nº: 0871 472-1884
Ticket Office: 0871 472-1884   Option 1
Website: www.dcfc.co.uk
E-mail: derby.county@dcfc.co.uk

GENERAL INFORMATION

Car Parking: Spaces for 1,424 cars at the ground (available for permit holders only). A further 200 spaces are available at Derby Conference Centre on London Road (£5.00 charge)
Coach Parking: At the ground
Nearest Railway Station: Derby (1 mile)
Nearest Bus Station: Derby Central
Club Shop: DCFC Megastore at the ground
Opening Times: Monday to Saturday 9.00am – 5.00pm (from 10.00am on Tuesdays); Sundays 10.00am – 4.00pm
Telephone Nº: 0871 472-1884 (Option 2)

GROUND INFORMATION

Away Supporters' Entrances & Sections:
South East Corner

ADMISSION INFO (2024/2025 PRICES)

Adult Seating: £33.00 – £37.00
Concessionary Seating: £25.00 – £28.00
Ages 13 to 17 Seating: £17.00 – £19.00
Ages 6 to 12 Seating: £9.00 – £10.00
Ages 2 to 5 Seating: £1.00

FANS WITH DISABILITIES INFORMATION

Wheelchairs: 206 spaces available in total
Helpers: One helper admitted for each fan with disabilities
Prices: Normal prices for disabled fans. Helpers free of charge
Disabled Toilets: Yes
Contact: (01332) 667528 Emma Drury   (Bookings are necessary) – emma.drury@dcfc.co.uk

Travelling Supporters' Information:
Routes: From All Parts: Exit the M1 at Junction 25 and follow the A52 towards the City Centre until the ground is signposted on the left. Follow the signs for the ground.
From the Train Station: The Stadium is 10 minutes walk by way of a tunnel under the railway opposite Brunswick Inn, Station Approach. Then follow the footpath; Buses: A shuttle service runs from the bus station from 1.00pm until 2.45pm on Saturdays. A similar service runs from 6.00pm – 7.30pm for midweek games. Return shuttles are available post-match.

HULL CITY AFC

Founded: 1904 (**Entered League**: 1905)
Nickname: 'Tigers'
Ground: MKM Stadium, West Park, Hull HU3 6HU
Ground Capacity: 25,586 (All seats)
Record Attendance: 25,030 (May 2010)

Colours: Black and Amber shirts with Black shorts
Telephone Nº: (01482) 504600
Ticket Office: (01482) 505600 (Weekdays only)
Website: www.wearehullcity.co.uk
E-mail: info@wearehullcity.co.uk

GENERAL INFORMATION

Car Parking: Walton Street Car Park (£5.00), City Centre Car Parks and a Park & Ride scheme from Priory Park (£1.20)
Coach Parking: By Police direction
Nearest Railway Station: Hull Paragon Interchange
Nearest Bus Station: City Centre, Hull
Club Shop: Tiger Leisure Superstore at the Stadium and in the Prospect Centre, Prince's Quay.
Opening Times: Superstore: Monday to Saturday 9.00am to 5.00pm and until 5.30pm on Saturday matchdays.
Prospect Centre: Monday to Saturday 9.00am to 5.30pm and Sunday 10.30am to 4.30pm.
Telephone Nº: (01482) 504600 or (01482) 358362

GROUND INFORMATION

Away Supporters' Entrances & Sections:
North Stand

ADMISSION INFO (2024/2025 PRICES)

Adult Seating: £20.00 – £28.00
Senior Citizen Seating: £13.50 – £18.00
Ages 16 to 22 Seating: £10.00 – £14.00
Ages 11 to 15 Seating: £7.00
Under-11s Seating: £3.00

FANS WITH DISABILITIES INFORMATION

Wheelchairs: 131 spaces in total for Home and Away fans available around all the stands at both upper and lower level
Helpers: One helper admitted per fan with disabilities (subject to registration)
Prices: Normal prices for fans with disabilities. Helpers free.
Disabled Toilets: Available throughout the ground.
Lifts are available. Commentaries are available for the blind
Contact: (01482) 358303   (Bookings are not necessary)
Disability Liaison Officer –
leanne.jensen@wearehullcity.co.uk

Travelling Supporters' Information:
Routes: From the West: Take the M62 then join the A63. Continue under the Humber Bridge as the road becomes the A63 Clive Sullivan Way and turn off at the slip road just before the flyover marked "Local Traffic/Infirmary". Take the 2nd exit at the roundabout into Rawling Way. Turn left at the next main set of traffic lights on A1105 Anlaby Road. Continue over the flyover then take a right turn into Walton Street. The car park is half way down this street after the Sports Arena; From the Humber Bridge: Follow signs for Hull City Centre – the road curves round to the left to join the A63 Clive Sullivan Way. Then as from the West; From the North: Take the A1079 towards Beverley then follow signs for the Humber Bridge and A164. Take the A63 sign-posted Hull City Centre and follow onto the A63 Clive Sullivan Way. Then as from the West.

33

LEEDS UNITED FC

Founded: 1919 (**Entered League**: 1920)
Former Names: Formed after Leeds City FC were wound up for 'Irregular Practices'
Nickname: 'United'
Ground: Elland Road, Leeds LS11 0ES
Ground Capacity: 37,890 (All seats)
Record Attendance: 57,892 (15th March 1967)

Colours: White shirts and shorts
Telephone Nº: 0871 334-1919
Ticket Office: 0871 334-1992
Website: www.leedsunited.com
E-mail: reception@leedsunited.com or
Supporters' Liaison – questions@leedsunited.com

GENERAL INFORMATION

Car Parking: Large car parks adjacent to the Stadium plus Park and Ride from Temple Green
Coach Parking: Adjacent to the Stadium
Nearest Railway Station: Leeds City (1½ miles)
Nearest Bus Station: Leeds City Centre – specials from Swinegate, Sovereign Street and also Pudsey Bus Station
Club Shop: At the Stadium, in the White Rose Shopping Centre, at Leeds/Bradford Airport and in central Leeds at the Merrion Centre and Trinity Leeds.
Opening Times: At the ground: Monday to Saturday 9.00am to 5.30pm and Sunday 10.00am to 4.00pm. Similar times in the central Leeds stores but with some variations. Generally open a little later and stay open a little later.
Telephone Nº: 0871 334-1919 (Option 5) at the Stadium or (0113) 242-5120 at the Merrion Centre

GROUND INFORMATION

Away Supporters' Entrances & Sections:
South East Corner or South Stand – Upper & Lower Tiers

ADMISSION INFO (2024/2025 PRICES)

Adult Seating: £32.00 – £49.00
Concessionary Seating: £25.00 – £34.00
Ages 16 to 18 Seating: £20.00 – £25.50
Under-16s Seating: £11.00 – £23.50
Note: Prices vary according to the category of game

FANS WITH DISABILITIES INFORMATION

Wheelchairs: 131 spaces in total in special sections in the West, North, South and East Stands
Helpers: One helper admitted per fan with disabilities
Prices: Concessionary prices are charged
Disabled Toilets: Available around the ground
Commentaries via headphones in the West Stand
Contact: (0113) 367-6178
(Bookings are necessary)
E-mail: disabledinfo@leedsunited.com

Travelling Supporters' Information:
Routes: From the North: Take the A58 or A61 into the City Centre and follow signs to the M621. Leave the Motorway after 1½ miles and exit the roundabout onto the A643 into Elland Road; From the North-East: Take the A63 or A64 into the City Centre (then as from the North); From the South: Take the M1 to the M621 (then as from the North); From the West: Take the M62 to the M621 (then as from the North).

LUTON TOWN FC

Founded: 1885 (**Re-entered League**: 2014)	**Record Attendance**: 30,069 (4th March 1959)
Former Names: The club was formed by the amalgamation of Wanderers FC and Excelsior FC	**Colours**: Orange shirts with Blue shorts
Nickname: 'Hatters'	**Telephone Nº**: (01582) 411622
	Ticket Office: (01582) 416976
Ground: Kenilworth Road Stadium, 1 Maple Road, Luton LU4 8AW	**Website**: www.lutontown.co.uk
	E-mail: info@lutontown.co.uk
Ground Capacity: 10,413 (All seats)	

GENERAL INFORMATION

Car Parking: Street parking is limited so the club recommends using Luton train station car park

Coach Parking: Luton Bus Station

Nearest Railway Station: Luton (1 mile)

Nearest Bus Station: Bute Street, Luton

Club Shop: Kenilworth Road Forecourt and also at Park Street in Luton town centre

Opening Times: 10.00am to 5.00pm

Telephone Nº: (01582) 411622 Option 4 (Park Street)

GROUND INFORMATION

Away Supporters' Entrances & Sections:
Oak Road for the Oak Stand

ADMISSION INFO (2024/2025 PRICES)

Note: Please contact the club for matchday admission prices as details were unavailable when we went to print.

FANS WITH DISABILITIES INFORMATION

Wheelchairs: 18 spaces for Home fans and 10 spaces for Away fans in the disabled section, Kenilworth Road End and Main Stand.

Helpers: One helper admitted per disabled person

Prices: Concessionary prices for the disabled. Helpers free

Disabled Toilets: Available adjacent to the disabled area

Contact: (01582) 411622 (Bookings are necessary)

Travelling Supporters' Information:

Routes: From the North and West: Exit the M1 at Junction 11 and follow signs for Luton (A505) into Dunstable Road. Follow the one-way system and turn right back towards Dunstable, take the second left into Ash Road for the ground; From the South and East: Exit the M1 at Junction 10 (or A6/A612) into Luton Town Centre and follow signs into Dunstable Road. After the railway bridge, take the sixth turning on the left into Ash Road for the ground.

MIDDLESBROUGH FC

Founded: 1876 (**Entered League**: 1899)
Nickname: 'Boro'
Ground: Riverside Stadium, Middlesbrough, TS3 6RS
Ground Capacity: 33,742 (All seats)
Record Attendance: 34,836 (28th December 2004)

Colours: Red shirts with White detailing, White shorts
Telephone Nº: (01642) 929420
Ticket Office: (01642) 929421
Website: www.mfc.co.uk
E-mail: reception@mfc.co.uk

GENERAL INFORMATION

Car Parking: 1,250 spaces available at the stadium – permit holders only. Otherwise use town centre parking.
Coach Parking: At the ground – Car Park D
Nearest Railway Station: Middlesbrough (½ mile)
Nearest Bus Station: Middlesbrough
Club Shops: At ground
Opening Times: Weekdays 9.00am to 5.00pm, Saturday Matchdays 9.00am to 3.00pm then 5.00pm to 6.00pm.
Telephone Nº: (01642) 929422

GROUND INFORMATION

Away Supporters' Entrances & Sections:
East Stand

ADMISSION INFO (2024/2025 PRICES)

Adult Seating: £26.00 – £37.00
Senior Citizen Seating: £17.00 – £29.00
Under-18s Seating: £12.00 – £22.00
Note: Prices depend on category of game

FANS WITH DISABILITIES INFORMATION

Wheelchairs: 81 spaces for home fans with 10 spaces for away fans in the East Stand
Helpers: One helper admitted per fan with disabilities
Prices: Normal prices for fans with disabilities. Helpers are admitted free of charge.
Disabled Toilets: Available in every stand with access via the Radar Key system
Contact: (01642) 929421 (Bookings are necessary) Rosemary Berks (DLO) – rosemary.berks@mfc.co.uk

Travelling Supporters' Information:
Routes: From the North: Take the A19 across the flyover and join the A66 (Eastbound). At the end of the flyover, turn left at North Ormesby where the ground is well-signposted. The ground is 200 metres down the road; From the South: Take the A1 and A19 to the junction with the A66 (Eastbound). After the flyover, turn left at North Ormesby following signs for the ground.

MILLWALL FC

Founded: 1885 (**Entered League**: 1920)
Former Names: Millwall Rovers FC (1885-1893); Millwall Athletic FC (1893-1925)
Nickname: 'The Lions'
Ground: The Den, Zampa Road, London SE16 3LN
Ground Capacity: 20,146 (All seats)

Record Attendance: 20,093 (10th January 1994)
Colours: Dark Blue shirts with White shorts
Telephone Nº: (020) 7232-1222
Ticket Office: (020) 7740-3470
Website: www.millwallfc.co.uk

GENERAL INFORMATION

Car Parking: Street parking
Coach Parking: Adjacent to the ground
Nearest Railway Station: New Cross Gate (1 mile), Surrey Quays (1 mile) or South Bermondsey (½ mile)
Nearest Tube: New Cross Gate (1 mile)/Canada Water (1 mile)
Club Shop: Next to the Stadium
Opening Times: Daily from 9.30am to 5.00pm
Telephone Nº: (020) 7231-9845

GROUND INFORMATION

Away Supporters' Entrances & Sections:
North Stand turnstiles 31-36. A walkway from South Bermondsey Station to the ground is open on matchdays

ADMISSION INFO (2024/2025 PRICES)

Adult Seating: £30.00 – £38.00
Under-18s Seating: £19.00 – £23.00
Under-16s Seating: £14.00 – £19.00
Under-12s Seating: £8.00 – £14.00 (**Under-6s**: £8.00)
Concessionary Seating: £24.00 – £27.00
Note: Prices vary depending on the category of the game

FANS WITH DISABILITIES INFORMATION

Wheelchairs: 36 spaces for home fans in the Barry Kitchener Stand plus 10 spaces for away fans in front of the North Stand
Helpers: One helper admitted per wheelchair
Prices: Standard prices for fans with disabilities. Helpers free
Disabled Toilets: 17 toilets available around the Stadium
Commentaries are available for the blind
Contact: (020) 7232-1222   (Bookings are necessary)
   slo@millwallplc.com

Travelling Supporters' Information:
Routes: From the North: Follow City signs from the M1/A1 then signs for Shoreditch & Whitechapel. Follow Ring Road signs for Dover, cross over Tower Bridge and after 1 mile take 1st exit at the roundabout onto the A2. From Elephant and Castle take the A2 (New Kent Road) into Old Kent Road and turn left after 4 miles into Ilderton Road to Zampa Road; From the South: Take the A20 & A21 following signs to London. At New Cross follow signs for Surrey Quays into Kender Street, turn left into Old Kent Road then right into Ilderton Road. Zampa Road is the 7th turning on the right; From the East: Take the A2 to New Cross (then as from the South); From the West: From M4 & M3 follow the South Circular (A205) then follow signs for Clapham, the City (A3) then Camberwell to New Cross and then as from South.

NORWICH CITY FC

Founded: 1902 (**Entered League**: 1920)
Nickname: 'Canaries'
Ground: Carrow Road, Norwich   NR1 1JE
Ground Capacity: 27,244 (All seats)
Record Attendance: 43,984 (30th March 1963)

Colours: Yellow shirts with Green shorts
Telephone Nº: (01603) 721902
Ticket Office: (01603) 721902 Option 1
Website: www.canaries.co.uk
E-mail: reception@canaries.co.uk

GENERAL INFORMATION

Car Parking: County Hall (NR1 2DW) and City Centre car parks are nearby
Coach Parking: Lower Clarence Road
Nearest Railway Station: Norwich Thorpe (1 mile)
Nearest Bus Station: Surrey Street, Norwich
Club Shop: At the ground and also stores in Chapelfield and the Castle Mall
Opening Times: Carrow Road store opens Monday to Saturday 9.00am to 5.30pm and Sunday 10.00am to 4.00pm. Chapelfield is open Monday to Saturday 9.00am to 6.00pm (until 8pm on Thursday and 7.00pm on Friday and Saturday), plus Sunday 11.00am to 5.00pm
Telephone Nº: (01603) 721902

GROUND INFORMATION

Away Supporters' Entrances & Sections:
South Stand using turnstiles 51-57

ADMISSION INFO (2024/2025 PRICES)

Adult Seating: £26.00 – £40.00
Senior Citizen Seating: £16.00 – £30.00
Under-18s Seating: £11.00 – £25.00
Under-12s Seating: £6.00 – £15.00

FANS WITH DISABILITIES INFORMATION

Wheelchairs: 84 spaces for home fans and 13 for away fans in the South Stand. Plenty of spaces are also available for ambulant fans with disabilities
Helpers: One helper admitted per fan with disabilities
Prices: Normal prices for fans with disabilities. Helpers free
Disabled Toilets: Available – Radar key operated
Contact: (01603) 721902   (Bookings are necessary) – stephen.graham@canaries.co.uk (Supporters' Liaison Officer)

Travelling Supporters' Information:
Routes: From the South: Take the A11 or A140 and turn right onto the A47 towards Great Yarmouth & Lowestoft, take the A146 Norwich/Lowestoft sliproad, turn left towards Norwich and follow road signs for the Football Ground; From the West: Take the A47 on to the A146 Norwich/Lowestoft slip road. Turn left towards Norwich, follow the road signs for the Football Ground.

OXFORD UNITED FC

Founded: 1893 (**Re-Entered League**: 2010)
Former Names: Headington United FC (1893-1960)
Nickname: 'U's'
Ground: Kassam Stadium, Grenoble Road, Oxford, OX4 4XP
Ground Capacity: 12,500 (All seats)

Record Attendance: 22,750 (At the Manor Ground)
Colours: Yellow shirts with Navy Blue shorts
Telephone Nº: (01865) 337500
Ticket Office: (01865) 337533
Website: www.oufc.co.uk

GENERAL INFORMATION

Car Parking: 2,000 free spaces available at the ground
Coach Parking: At the ground
Nearest Railway Station: Oxford (4 miles)
Nearest Bus Station: Oxford
Club Shop: At the ground and also in the Covered Market in Oxford city centre
Opening Times: Monday to Friday 10.00am to 5.00pm and Matchdays from 10.00am until kick-off at the ground. The Covered Market shop opens Tuesday to Friday 9.00am to 5.00pm and Saturday 10.00am to 4.00pm.
Telephone Nº: (01865) 747231 (at the ground)

GROUND INFORMATION

Away Supporters' Entrances & Sections:
North Stand turnstiles for North Stand accommodation. Ticket office for away supporters is adjacent

ADMISSION INFO (2024/2025 PRICES)

Adult Seating: £23.00 – £35.00
Senior Citizen Seating: £16.00 – £29.00
Ages 18 to 24 Seating: £15.00 – £28.00
Under-18s Seating: £10.00 – £26.00
Under-13s Seating: £7.00 – £20.00
Under-7s Seating: £7.00 – £16.00 (Free with a paying adult in the Family Area)

FANS WITH DISABILITIES INFORMATION

Wheelchairs: Accommodated in areas in the North, East and South Stands
Helpers: One assistant admitted per fan with disabilities
Prices: Normal prices for fans with disabilities. One assistant also admitted free of charge if required
Disabled Toilets: Available throughout the ground
Contact: (01865) 337533 (Bookings are necessary)

Travelling Supporters' Information:
Routes: From the Oxford Ring Road take the A4074 towards Henley and Reading then turn left after ½ mile following signs for the Oxford Science Park. Bear left and go straight on at two roundabouts then the Stadium is on the left in Grenoble Road. The Kassam Stadium is clearly signposted on all major roads in Oxford.

PLYMOUTH ARGYLE FC

Founded: 1886 (**Entered League**: 1920)
Former Names: Argyle FC (1886-1903)
Nickname: 'Pilgrims' 'Argyle'
Ground: Home Park, Plymouth   PL2 3DQ
Ground Capacity: 17,904 (All seats)
Record Attendance: 43,596 (10th October 1936)

Colours: Green shirts and White shorts
Telephone Nº: (01752) 562561
Ticket Office: (01752) 907700
Website: www.pafc.co.uk
E-mail: argyle@pafc.co.uk

GENERAL INFORMATION

Car Parking: Car park for 1,000 cars is adjacent
Coach Parking: Central Park Car Park
Nearest Railway Station: Plymouth North Road
Nearest Bus Station: Coach hub off Mayflower Street
Club Shop: At the ground
Opening Times: Monday to Friday 9.00am to 5.00pm, Saturday home matchdays 9.00am to 3.00pm plus 30 minutes after the game. Saturday away matchdays 10.00am to 1.00pm.
Telephone Nº: (01752) 562561

GROUND INFORMATION

Away Supporters' Entrances & Sections:
Barn Park End turnstiles for Blocks 22/23 (covered seating)

ADMISSION INFO (2024/2025 PRICES)

Adult Seating: £23.00 - £28.00
Senior Citizen/Under-23s Seating: £19.00 – £23.00
Under-18s Seating: £9.00 – £11.00
Under-14s Seating: £6.00 – £8.00
Under-8s Seating: £2.00 – £3.00
Note: Tickets are cheaper if purchased before the matchday and Family Tickets are also available.

FANS WITH DISABILITIES INFORMATION

Wheelchairs: 80 spaces Home fans and 28 spaces for Away fans at pitch level
Helpers: One helper admitted per fan with disabilities
Prices: Normal prices apply for fans with disabilities. Helpers are admitted free of charge
Disabled Toilets: Available throughout the stadium
Commentaries are available for the visually impaired
Contact: (01752) 562561   disability@pafc.co.uk
(Bookings are necessary)

Travelling Supporters' Information:
Routes: From All Parts: Take the A38 to Tavistock Road (A386), then branch left following signs for Home Park (A386) and continue for 1¼ miles. The car park for the ground is on the left (signposted Home Park).

PORTSMOUTH FC

Founded: 1898 (**Entered League**: 1920)
Nickname: 'Pompey'
Ground: Fratton Park, 57 Frogmore Road, Portsmouth, Hants PO4 8RA
Ground Capacity: 19,669 (All seats)
Record Attendance: 51,385 (26th February 1949)

Colours: Blue shirts with White shorts
Telephone Nº: 0345 646-1898
Ticket Office: 0345 646-1898
Website: www.portsmouthfc.co.uk
E-mail: info@pompeyfc.co.uk

GENERAL INFORMATION

Car Parking: Street parking plus a limited number of spaces at Fratton Park (first come, first served – £10.00 charge)
Coach Parking: By Police direction
Nearest Railway Station: Fratton (adjacent)
Nearest Bus Station: The Hard, Portsmouth
Club Shop: At the ground in Anson Road (North Stand)
Opening Times: Monday to Friday 9.00am – 5.30pm. Saturday and Weekday Matchdays 9.00am until half-time.
Telephone Nº: (023) 9421-1270

GROUND INFORMATION

Away Supporters' Entrances & Sections:
Apsley Road – Milton Road side for Apsley Road End

ADMISSION INFO (2024/2025 PRICES)

Adult Seating: £28.00
Senior Citizen Seating: £22.00
Ages 18 to 22 Seating: £19.00
Ages 14 to 17 Seating: £11.00
Ages 2 to 13 Seating: £6.00
Note: Adults, Senior Citizens or Ages 17 to 22 must be accompanied by a Junior to sit in the Family Section.

FANS WITH DISABILITIES INFORMATION

Wheelchairs: 58 spaces available in total in a special section in the Fratton End including 5 spaces for away fans
Helpers: One helper admitted per fan with disabilities
Prices: Wheelchair users are charged £18.00 and ambulant fans with disabilities are charged £20.00. Free for helpers
Disabled Toilets: One available in disabled section (Radar Key required for access)
Contact: 0345 646-1898 (Bookings are necessary) – emmasmith@pompeyfc.co.uk (Disability Liaison Officer)

Travelling Supporters' Information:
Routes: From the North and West: Take the M27 and M275 to the end then take the 2nd exit at the roundabout and after ¼ mile turn right at the 'T' junction into London Road (A2047). After 1¼ miles cross the railway bridge and turn left into Goldsmith Avenue. After ½ mile turn left into Frogmore Road; From the East: Take the A27 following Southsea signs (A2030). Turn left at the roundabout (3 miles) onto the A288, then right into Priory Crescent and next right into Carisbrooke Road for the ground.

PRESTON NORTH END FC

Founded: 1880 (**Entered League**: 1888)
Nickname: 'Lilywhites' 'North End'
Ground: Deepdale, Sir Tom Finney Way, Preston, PR1 6RU
Ground Capacity: 23,404 (All seats)
Record Attendance: 42,684 (23rd April 1938)

Colours: White shirts with Blue shorts
Telephone N°: 0344 856-1964
Ticket Office: 0344 856-1966
Website: www.pnefc.net
E-mail: enquiries@pne.com

GENERAL INFORMATION

Car Parking: Four official car parks at the stadium plus further parking at Moor Park School
Coach Parking: By prior arrangement with the club
Nearest Railway Station: Preston (2 miles)
Nearest Bus Station: Preston (1 mile)
Club Shop: At the ground
Opening Times: Monday to Saturday 9.00am to 5.00pm and midweek matchdays 9.00am until kick-off
Telephone N°: 0344 856-1965

GROUND INFORMATION

Away Supporters' Entrances & Sections:
Bill Shankly Kop

ADMISSION INFO (2024/2025 PRICES)

Adult Seating: £30.00 – £35.00
Senior Citizen Seating: £25.00 – £30.00
Ages 19 to 22 Seating: £20.00 – £25.00
Ages 11 to 18 Seating: £7.50 – £20.00
Under-11s Seating: £5.00 – £10.00
Note: Discounted Family Tickets are also available

FANS WITH DISABILITIES INFORMATION

Wheelchairs: 160 spaces are available for advance order
Helpers: One helper admitted per fan with disabilities
Prices: Normal prices for fans with disabilities. Helpers free
Disabled Toilets: Available throughout the ground
Commentaries are available for the blind
Contact: (01772) 693324 (Bookings are usually necessary)
Lucy Stephenson (DLO) – lucy@pne.com (0344) 856 1966

Travelling Supporters' Information:
Routes: From the North: Take the M6 then the M55 to Junction 1. Follow signs for Preston (A6). After 2 miles turn left at the crossroads into Blackpool Road (A5085). Turn right ¾ mile into Deepdale; From the South and East: Exit the M6 at Junction 31 and follow Preston signs (A59). Take the 2nd exit at the roundabout (1 mile) into Blackpool Road. Turn left after 1¼ miles into Deepdale; From the West: Exit the M55 at Junction 1 (then as from the North).

QUEEN'S PARK RANGERS FC

Founded: 1882 (**Entered League**: 1920)	**Record Attendance**: 35,353 (27th April 1974)
Former Names: Formed by the amalgamation of St. Jude's FC and Christchurch Rangers FC	**Colours**: Blue and White hooped shirts, White shorts
Nickname: 'Rangers' 'R's'	**Telephone Nº**: (020) 8743-0262
Ground: Matrade Loftus Road Stadium,	**Ticket Office**: (020) 8740-2613
South Africa Road, London W12 7PJ	**Website**: www.qpr.co.uk
Ground Capacity: 18,181 (All seats)	**E-mail**: boxoffice@qpr.co.uk

GENERAL INFORMATION

Car Parking: Street parking
Coach Parking: By Police direction
Nearest Railway Station: Shepherd's Bush
Nearest Tube Station: White City (Central) or Wood Lane (Hammersmith & City)
Club Shop: Superstore at the ground
Opening Times: Weekdays 9.00am to 5.00pm. Weekday matchdays until 15 minutes before kick-off. Non-match Saturdays 9.00am to 5.00pm. Saturday matchdays 9.00am until 15 minutes before kick-off then 45 minutes after game (but not for evening matches)
Telephone Nº: (020) 8749-6862

GROUND INFORMATION

Away Supporters' Entrances & Sections:

Access via South Africa Road turnstile 2 for School End Lower and Ellerslie Road turnstile 13 for School End Upper

ADMISSION INFO (2024/2025 PRICES)

Adult Seating: £26.00 – £47.00
Senior Citizen/Ages 18 to 23 Seating: £19.00 – £36.00
Under-18s Seating: £16.00 – £32.00
Under-8s Seating (Accompanied): Free – £21.00
Note: Prices shown are for matchday ticket purchases. Discounts are available to members and for advance purchases

FANS WITH DISABILITIES INFORMATION

Wheelchairs: 24 spaces available
Helpers: One helper admitted per wheelchair
Prices: £19.00 - £28.00 for fans with disabilities. Free of charge for helpers
Disabled Toilets: Available
Commentaries for the blind are available in the Ellerslie Road Stand. Please contact the Ticket Office to arrange this facility.
Contact: (020) 8740-2613   (Bookings are necessary)
boxoffice@qpr.co.uk

Travelling Supporters' Information:
Routes: From the North: Take the M1 & M406 North Circular for Neasden, go left after ¾ mile (A404) following signs for Harlesden, Hammersmith, past White City Stadium, right into White City Road and left into South Africa Road; From the South: Take A206 then A3 across Putney Bridge and follow signs to Hammersmith then Oxford (A219) to Shepherd's Bush. Join the A4020 following signs to Acton, turn right (¼ mile) into Loftus Road; From the East: Take the A12, A406 then the A503 to join the Ring Road, follow Oxford signs and join the A40(M), branch left (2 miles) to the M41, take the 3rd exit at the roundabout to the A4020 (then as South); From the West: Take the M4 to Chiswick then the A315 & A402 to Shepherd's Bush, join A4020 (then as South).

SHEFFIELD UNITED FC

Founded: 1889 (**Entered League**: 1892)
Nickname: 'Blades'
Ground: Bramall Lane, Sheffield   S2 4SU
Ground Capacity: 32,125 (All seats)
Record Attendance: 68,287 (15th February 1936)

Colours: Red and White striped shirts, Black shorts
Telephone Nº: (0114) 253-7200
Ticket Office: (0114) 253-7200
Website: www.sufc.co.uk
E-mail: info@sufc.co.uk

GENERAL INFORMATION

Car Parking: Street parking only
Coach Parking: By Police direction
Nearest Railway Station: Sheffield Midland (1 mile)
Nearest Bus Station: Pond Street, Sheffield (1 mile)
Club Shop: At the ground
Opening Times: Monday to Friday 9.00am to 5.00pm (until kick-off on matchdays). Saturdays 9.00am to 4.00pm (until 3.00pm and then for 30 minutes after the game on matchdays)
Telephone Nº: (0114) 253-7200

GROUND INFORMATION

Away Supporters' Entrances & Sections:
Redbrik – Bramall Lane Stand Lower Tier

ADMISSION INFO (2024/2025 PRICES)

Adult Seating: From £30.00
Senior Citizen Seating: From £20.00
Under-22s/Student Seating: From £20.00
Under-18s Seating: From £2.00
Junior Seating: From £12.00

FANS WITH DISABILITIES INFORMATION

Wheelchairs: 95 spaces available for home fans along with 10 spaces for away fans in the Westfield Corner Stand
Helpers: One helper admitted per wheelchair
Prices: Concessionary prices for fans with disabilities. Free of charge for helpers
Disabled Toilets: 12 available within the enclosure
Commentaries available for the blind on request
Contact: (0114) 253-7200   (Bookings are necessary)

Travelling Supporters' Information:
Routes: From the North: Exit the M1 at Junction 33 following signs to Sheffield (A57) and continue along Sheffield Parkway until the Park Square roundabout. Take the 3rd exit and follow the A61 (Sheffield). Midland Station is on the left, the road veers to the left then take the middle lane following the ring road to the right. Take the first exit at the roundabout into Bramhall Lane.; From the South: Exit the M1 at junction 29 and take the A617 (Chesterfield). Take the 3rd exit at the roundabout onto the A61 and continue to the Earl of Arundel and Surrey Public House. Turn left and continue into Bramhall Lane; From the East: Exit the M1 at Junctions 31 or 33 and take the A57 to the roundabout, take the 3rd exit into Sheaf Street (then as from the North); From the West: Take the A57 into Sheffield and take the 4th exit at the roundabout into Upper Hanover Street and at the 2nd roundabout take the 3rd exit into Bramall Lane.

SHEFFIELD WEDNESDAY FC

Founded: 1867 (**Entered League**: 1892)
Former Name: The Wednesday FC
Nickname: 'Owls'
Ground: Hillsborough, Sheffield   S6 1SW
Ground Capacity: 34,835 (All seats)
Record Attendance: 72,841 (17th February 1934)

Colours: Blue and White striped shirts, Black shorts
Telephone Nº: 03700 20-1867
Ticket Hotline: 03700 20-1867 Option 1
Website: www.swfc.co.uk
E-mail: mediaenquiries@swfc.co.uk

GENERAL INFORMATION

Car Parking: Street parking plus private car parks around the stadium
Coach Parking: Clay Wheels Lane
Nearest Railway Station: Sheffield Midland (4 miles)
Nearest Bus Station: Pond Street, Sheffield (4 miles)
Club Shop: At the ground
Ground Opening Times: Monday to Friday from 9.00am to 5.00pm and non-match Saturdays from 9.00am to 12.00pm. Saturdays matchdays 9.00am to 3.00pm then 45 minutes after the game.
Telephone Nº: 03700 20-1867

GROUND INFORMATION

Away Supporters' Entrances & Sections:
Leppings Lane turnstiles for the West Stand, Upper Tier

ADMISSION INFO (2024/2025 PRICES)

Adult Seating: £30.00 – £54.00
Concessionary Seating: £20.00 – £44.00
Ages 12 to 17 Seating: £15.00 – £20.00
Under-11s Seating: £10.00 – £15.00
Under-5s Seating: £5.00

FANS WITH DISABILITIES INFORMATION

Wheelchairs: 91 spaces for home fans and 9 spaces for visiting fans in special sections in the North Stand, Kop Stand and West Stand Lower. Ambulant fans with disabilities can sit in any section of the ground other than the Grandstand.
Helpers: Admitted
Prices: Normal prices for the disabled. Helpers free of charge
Disabled Toilets: Available in the North and West Stands Commentaries are available for the blind
Contact: dlo@swfc.co.uk   (Bookings are necessary)

Travelling Supporters' Information:
Routes: From the North, South and East: Exit the M1 at Junction 36 and follow signs to Sheffield (A61). Continue for 4 miles then take the 3rd exit at the 2nd roundabout into Leppings Lane. The ground is situated on the left; From the West: Take the A57 until the road splits in two. Take the left fork (A6101). After 3¾ miles turn left onto the one-way system and follow the road round to the right onto Holme Lane. This road becomes Bradfield Road. At the junction with the A61 (Penistone Road), turn left towards Barnsley. The stadium is on the left after Hillsborough Park.

STOKE CITY FC

Founded: 1863 (**Entered League**: 1888)
Former Name: Stoke FC
Nickname: 'The Potters'
Ground: bet365 Stadium, Stanley Matthews Way,
Stoke-on-Trent ST4 4EG
Ground Capacity: 30,089 (All seats)

Record Attendance: 30,022 (17th March 2018)
Colours: Red and White striped shirts, White shorts
Telephone Nº: (01782) 367598 or (01782) 592233
Ticket Office: (01782) 367599
Website: www.stokecityfc.com
E-mail: info@stokecityfc.com

GENERAL INFORMATION

Car Parking: At the ground (bookings necessary). Also various car parks within 10 minutes walk
Coach Parking: At the ground
Nearest Railway Station: Stoke-on-Trent (1½ miles)
Nearest Bus Station: Glebe Street, Stoke-on-Trent
Club Shop: At the ground and at the Potteries Shopping Centre in Hanley
Opening Times: Weekdays 9.00am–5.30pm, non-match Saturdays 9.00am–2.00pm. Weekend Matchdays 9.00am to kick-off then 30 minutes after the final whistle. Evening games 9.00am to kick-off and 30 minutes after the game. Potteries Store: Monday to Saturday 9.00am–6.00pm (until 8.00pm on Thursday) and Sunday 10.30am to 4.30pm.
Telephone Nº: (01782) 592242 (shop at the ground) and (01782) 592132 (Potteries shop)

GROUND INFORMATION

Away Supporters' Sections: South Stand

ADMISSION INFO (2024/2025 PRICES)

Adult Seating: £20.00 – £40.00
Senior Citizen Seating: £15.00 – £32.00
Under-17s Seating: £12.00 – £23.00
Under-11s Seating: £10.00 – £19.00
Note: Prices vary depending on the category of the game

FANS WITH DISABILITIES INFORMATION

Wheelchairs: 186 spaces available for home fans and 26 spaces available for away fans
Helpers: One helper admitted per disabled person
Prices: Concessionary prices for disabled fan. Helpers free
Disabled Toilets: Available
Commentaries are available – phone for details
Contact: (01782) 367598   (Bookings are necessary)
or e-mail accessibility@stokecityfc.com

Travelling Supporters' Information:
Routes: From the North, South and West: Exit the M6 at Junction 15 and take the A500 to Stoke-on-Trent then the A50 towards Derby/Uttoxeter (the bet365 Stadium is signposted and visible to the right). Once on the A50 take the fist exit, turn right at the traffic lights and cross over the flyover. Turn right at the first roundabout, left at the next roundabout and right at the third roundabout for the stadium; From the East: Take the A50 to Stoke-on-Trent and take the last turn-off (signposted for bet365 Stadium). Go straight on at the first roundabout then right at the second roundabout to reach the stadium.

SUNDERLAND AFC

Founded: 1879 (**Entered League**: 1890)
Former Names: Sunderland and District Teachers FC
Nickname: 'The Black Cats'
Ground: Stadium of Light, Sunderland   SR5 1SU
Ground Capacity: 48,707 (All seats)
Record Attendance: 48,353 (13th April 2002)

Colours: Red and White striped shirts, Black shorts
Telephone Nº: 0371 911-1200
Ticket Office: 0371 911-1973
Website: www.safc.com
E-mail: enquiries@safc.com

GENERAL INFORMATION

Car Parking: Park and Ride from Wessington Way (SR5 3XG)
Coach Parking: At the ground – must be pre-booked
Nearest Railway Station: Sunderland (1 mile)
Nearest Bus Station: Town Centre (1 mile)
Club Shop: At the Stadium, plus smaller stores at Debenhams in Sunderland
Opening Times: Monday to Saturday 9.00am – 5.30pm and Sunday 10.00am to 4.00pm
Telephone Nº: (0191) 551-5375

GROUND INFORMATION

Away Supporters' Entrances & Sections:
Carling North Stand (Upper Tier)

ADMISSION INFO (2024/2025 PRICES)

Adult Seating: £29.00 – £36.00
Senior Citizen Seating: £22.00 – £29.00
Under-22s Seating: £22.00 – £24.00
Under-16s Seating: £12.00 – £14.00
Note: Limited availability so please check with the club.

FANS WITH DISABILITIES INFORMATION

Wheelchairs: 202 spaces in total throughout the stadium
Helpers: Admitted
Prices: Normal prices for fans with disabilities. Helpers free
Disabled Toilets: Available in all stands and Corporate areas
Contact: 0371 911-1200   (Bookings are necessary) – chris.waters@safc.com (Disability Liaison Officer)

Travelling Supporters' Information:
Routes: From All Parts: Exit the A1 at the A690 Durham/Sunderland exit. After approximately 4 miles turn left onto the A19 (signposted Tyne Tunnel). Keep in the left lane and take the slip road (signposted Washington/Sunderland) onto the bridge over the River Wear. Turn right onto the A1231 (signposted Washington/Sunderland), stay on this road going straight across 4 roundabouts into Sunderland. Continue straight through 2 sets of traffic lights and the Stadium car park is on the right, about 1 mile past the traffic lights.

SWANSEA CITY FC

Founded: 1912 (**Entered League**: 1920)
Former Name: Swansea Town FC (1912-1970)
Nickname: 'The Swans'
Ground: Swansea.com Stadium, Landore, Swansea, SA1 2FA
Ground Capacity: 21,000 (All seats)

Record Attendance: 32,796 (at the Vetch Field)
Colours: White and Black shirts, shorts and socks
Telephone Nº: (01792) 616400
Ticket Office: (01792) 616400 Option 1
Website: www.swanseacity.com
E-mail: info@swanseacityfc.co.uk

GENERAL INFORMATION

Car Parking: Reserved parking only at the stadium but 3,000 spaces are available in a Park & Ride scheme just off Junction 45 of the M4.
Coach Parking: By Police direction
Nearest Railway Station: Swansea High Street (1½ miles)
Nearest Bus Station: Quadrant Depot (2½ miles)
Club Shop: At the ground
Opening Times: Monday to Friday 10.00am to 5.00pm, Saturday from 9.00am to 5.00pm and Sunday 10.00am to 4.00pm
Telephone Nº: (01792) 616546

GROUND INFORMATION

Away Supporters' Entrances & Sections:
North Stand

ADMISSION INFO (2024/2025 PRICES)

Adult Seating: £23.50 – £32.50
Concessionary Seating: £15.50 – £20.00
Under-18s Seating: £10.50 – £14.50
Under-12s Seating: £6.00 – £9.50

FANS WITH DISABILITIES INFORMATION

Wheelchairs: 135 spaces available for home fans and helpers and 15 spaces available for away fans and helpers
Helpers: One helper admitted per wheelchair
Prices: Normal prices apply for fans with disabilities. Free of charge for helpers
Disabled Toilets: Available
There are a number of disabled parking spaces available at the stadium
Contact: (01792) 616611 (Bookings are necessary)

Travelling Supporters' Information:
Routes: From All Parts: Exit the M4 at Junction 45 and follow signs for Swansea (A4067). The stadium is clearly signposted.

WATFORD FC

Founded: 1881 (**Entered League**: 1920)
Former Names: Formed by the amalgamation of
West Herts FC and St. Mary's FC
Nickname: 'Hornets'
Ground: Vicarage Road Stadium, Watford, WD18 0ER
Ground Capacity: 21,577 (All seats)
Record Attendance: 34,099 (3rd February 1969)

Colours: Yellow & Black striped shirts, Black shorts
Telephone Nº: (01923) 223023
Ticket Office: (01923) 223023
Website: www.watfordfc.com
E-mail: yourvoice@watfordfc.com

GENERAL INFORMATION

Car Parking: Nearby multi-storey car parks and schools
Coach Parking: By Police direction
Nearest Railway Station: Watford Junction or Watford
Tube Station (Metropolitan Line)
Nearest Bus Station: Watford Town Centre
Club Shop: The Hornets Shop at Vicarage Road Stadium
and at Intu Watford
Opening Times: Monday to Saturday 9.00am to 6.00pm at
the stadium. Intu Watford: Monday to Wednesday 9.00am
to 6.00pm , Thursday to Saturday 9.00am to 8.00pm and
Sunday 11.00am to 5.00pm
Telephone Nº: (01923) 496000

GROUND INFORMATION

Away Supporters' Entrances & Sections:
Vicarage Road End entrances and accommodation

ADMISSION INFO (2024/2025 PRICES)

Adult Seating: £25.00 – £33.00
Senior Citizen Seating: £15.00 – £21.00
Ages 19 to 21 Seating: £12.00 – £18.00
Under-18s Seating: £5.00 – £10.00

FANS WITH DISABILITIES INFORMATION

Wheelchairs: 151 spaces in total in accessible platforms
located in all 4 stands.
Prices and Helpers: Normal prices for fans with disabilities.
One assistant is admitted free with each fan with disabilities
Disabled Toilets: Available
Commentaries available around the ground – no charge
Contact: (01923) 223023   (Bookings in advance helpful)
E-mail: disabled.supporters@watfordfc.com

Travelling Supporters' Information:
Routes: Vicarage Road is closed to traffic from 2 hours before kick-off on matchday. The following directions lead to the nearest
car park: From the North and East: Exit the M25 at Junction 20 and take the first exit onto the A41. At the next roundabout,
take the second exit onto A411 (Hempstead Road). * Continue along the A411 to the town centre. At the large roundabout take
the second exit feeding into the inner ring road, which is a one-way system. Stay in the righthand lane and follow the Ring Road
until you see the entrance to the Church car park on your right hand side; From the South and West: Exit the M25 at Junction
19 then take the third exit at the roundabout onto A411 (Hempstead Road). Then as from * above; From Central London: Exit
the M1 Junction 5 and take the second exit onto the A4008. Cross the first roundabout, then take the second exit at the next
towards the town centre. At the traffic lights, turn left onto the inner ring road at the T-junction and filter across to the right-
hand lane. Follow the Ring Road until you see the entrance to the Church car park on your right hand side.

WEST BROMWICH ALBION FC

Founded: 1879 (**Entered League**: 1888)
Former Name: West Bromwich Strollers (1879-1880)
Nickname: 'Throstles' 'Baggies' 'Albion'
Ground: The Hawthorns, Halfords Lane,
West Bromwich, West Midlands   B71 4LF
Ground Capacity: 26,850 (All seats)
Record Attendance: 64,815 (6th March 1937)

Colours: Navy Blue & White striped shirts with
White shorts
Telephone Nº: (0121) 227-2227
Ticket Office: (0121) 227-2227
Website: www.wba.co.uk
E-mail: enquiries@wbafc.co.uk

GENERAL INFORMATION

Car Parking: Halfords Lane Car Parks, East Stand Car Park and several independent car parks
Coach Parking: At the ground
Nearest Railway Station: Hawthorns (200 yards) or Rolfe Street, Smethwick (1½ miles)
Nearest Midland Metro: Hawthorns (200 yards)
Nearest Bus Station: West Bromwich Town Centre
Club Shop: At the ground and at the Merry Hill Centre
Opening Times: Weekdays 9.00am – 5.00pm, Saturday Matchdays 9.00am – 2.45pm and Sundays 10.00am – 2.00pm Merryhill Centre: Monday to Saturday 10.00am to 4.00pm and Sunday 11.00am to 5.00pm
Telephone Nº: 0871 271-9790 (Stadium Megastore), 0871 271-9793 (Merry Hill Centre)

GROUND INFORMATION

Away Supporters' Entrances & Sections:
Smethwick End 'A' turnstiles

ADMISSION INFO (2024/2025 PRICES)

Adult Seating: £30.00
Concessionary Seating: £25.00
Ages 20 to 25 Seating: £20.00
Ages 17 to 19 Seating: £14.00
Under-17s Seating: £5.00

FANS WITH DISABILITIES INFORMATION

Wheelchairs: 171 spaces in total in special sections in the Birmingham Road End, Smethwick End and East Stand
Helpers: One helper admitted with each fan with disabilities (subject to availability of space)
Prices: £20.00 for fans with disabilities. Helpers free
Disabled Toilets: 14 in total available around the ground
Contact: (0121) 227-2227 (Bookings are necessary) – Liz Massey (DLO) – liz.massey@wbafc.co.uk

Travelling Supporters' Information:
Routes: From All Parts: Exit the M5 at Junction 1 and follow Matchday signs for the ground. The matchday traffic plan has made the "obvious" route via the A41 unusable for home games.

EFL League One

Website www.efl.com

Email info@efltrust.com

Clubs for the 2024/2025 Season

BARNSLEY FC

Founded: 1887 (**Entered League**: 1898)
Former Names: Barnsley St. Peter's
Nickname: 'The Tykes' 'Reds'
Ground: Oakwell Stadium, Barnsley   S71 1ET
Ground Capacity: 23,287 (All seats)
Record Attendance: 40,255 (15th February 1936)

Colours: Red shirts with White shorts and Red socks
Telephone Nº: (01226) 211211
Ticket Office: (01226) 211183
Website: www.barnsleyfc.co.uk
E-mail: via club website

GENERAL INFORMATION

Car Parking: Queen's Ground Car Park (adjacent)
Coach Parking: Queen's Ground Car Park
Nearest Railway Station: Barnsley Interchange (6 minutes walk)
Nearest Bus Station: Barnsley Interchange
Club Shop: At the Stadium
Opening Times: Please contact the club for details due to uncertainty caused by the pandemic.
Telephone Nº: (01226) 211400

GROUND INFORMATION

Away Supporters' Entrances & Sections:
Palmer Construction North Stand Turnstiles 42-51

ADMISSION INFO (2024/2025 PRICES)

Adult Seating: £27.00 – £29.00
Concessionary Seating: £20.00 – £22.00
Under-19s Seating: £14.00
Under-14s Seating: £9.00
Note: Prices are lower for tickets purchased in advance

FANS WITH DISABILITIES INFORMATION

Wheelchairs: 60 wheelchair spaces available in total in designated disabled areas including 18 spaces for Away fans in the North Stand.
Helpers: Admitted
Prices: Normal prices for fans with disabilities but helpers are admitted free of charge
Disabled Toilets: Available in the Corner Stand, and the Barry Murphy North Stand.
Commentaries are available for the blind
Contact: (01266) 211183   (Bookings are necessary) – (Disability Liaison Officer)

Travelling Supporters' Information: From All Parts: Exit the M1 at Junction 37 and follow the 'Barnsley FC/Football Ground' signs which lead to a large surface car park adjacent to the stadium (2 miles).

BIRMINGHAM CITY FC

Founded: 1875 (**Entered League**: 1892)
Former Names: Small Heath Alliance FC (1875-88); Small Heath FC (1888-1905); Birmingham FC (1905-45)
Nickname: 'The Blues'
Ground: St. Andrew's Stadium, Cattell Road, St. Andrew's, Birmingham   B9 4RL
Ground Capacity: 29,409 (All seats)

Record Attendance: 68,844 (11th March 1939)
Colours: Shirts are Royal Blue with White sleeves, White shorts
Telephone N°: (0121) 772-0101
Ticket Office: (0121) 772-0101 (Option 2)
Website: www.bcfc.com
E-mail: reception@bcfc.com

GENERAL INFORMATION

Car Parking: Street Parking + Birmingham Wheels (secure parking but not related to the club)
Coach Parking: Coventry Road
Nearest Railway Station: Birmingham New Street or Birmingham Moor Street (20 minutes walk)
Nearest Bus Station: Digbeth National Express Coach Station
Club Shops: Blues Store at the ground
Opening Times: Monday to Saturday 9.00am to 5.00pm. Matchdays open from 9.00am until kick-off then for a further 30 minutes after the game. Sundays 10.30am to 4.30pm.
Telephone N°: (0121) 772-0101 (Option 4)

GROUND INFORMATION

Away Supporters' Entrances & Sections:
Gil Merrick Stand, Coventry Road

ADMISSION INFO (2024/2025 PRICES)

Adult Seating: £22.50 – £35.00
Concessionary Seating: £17.50 – £27.50
Ages 16 to 22 Seating: £17.50 – £22.50
Under-16s Seating: £5.00 – £20.00
Note: Prices vary depending on the category of the match and the location of the seat.

FANS WITH DISABILITIES INFORMATION

Wheelchairs: 88 spaces in total (including 21 for Away fans) in the Spion Kop Stand, Gil Merrick Lower Stand, Tilton Road Stand and East Paddocks
Helpers: One assistant admitted for each fan with disabilities
Prices: Normal prices apply for fans with disabilities. Helpers are admitted free of charge
Disabled Toilets: 14 available in the Spion Kop Stand, Family Stand, Gil Merrick Stand and Tilton Road Stand
Contact: (0121) 772-0101 Option 2 (Bookings are necessary)

Travelling Supporters' Information: From All Parts: Exit M6 at Junction 6 and take the A38 (M) (Aston Expressway). Leave at 2nd exit then take first exit at roundabout along the Dartmouth Middleway. After 1¼ miles turn left on to Coventry Road.
Bus Services: Services 17, 58, 59 & 60 from Birmingham Centre stop at Cattell Road just to the south of the stadium and Services 97f stops at Garrison Lane just to the north of the stadium.

BLACKPOOL FC

Founded: 1887 (**Entered League**: 1896)
Former Name: Merged with Blackpool St. Johns (1887)
Nickname: 'Seasiders' or 'Tangerines'
Ground: Bloomfield Road, Blackpool, FY1 6JJ
Ground Capacity: 16,616 (All seats)
Record Attendance: 38,098 (17th September 1955)

Colours: Tangerine shirts with White shorts
Telephone Nº: (01253) 599344
Ticket Office: (01253) 599745
Website: www.blackpoolfc.co.uk
E-mail: tickets@blackpoolfc.co.uk

GENERAL INFORMATION

Car Parking: 3,000 spaces at the ground and street parking
Coach Parking: Available at the ground
Nearest Railway Station: Blackpool South (5 mins. walk)
Nearest Bus Station: Talbot Road (2 miles)
Club Shop: At the ground
Opening Times: Weekdays 9.00am to 5.00pm (until kick-off on Tuesday matchdays). Saturdays 9.00am to 12.00pm but until kick-off and for 30 minutes after the game on Saturday matchdays.
Telephone Nº: (01253) 599745

GROUND INFORMATION

Away Supporters' Entrances & Sections:
North Side entrances for the East Stand (temporary)

ADMISSION INFO (2024/2025 PRICES)

Adult Seating: £23.00 – £40.00
Senior Citizen/Ages 18 to 21 Seating: £20.00 – £40.00
Under-18s Seating: £12.00 – £35.00
Under-14s Seating: £8.00 – £35.00
Under-5s Seating: Free to £35.00

FANS WITH DISABILITIES INFORMATION

Wheelchairs: Over 50 spaces in total for home and away fans
Helpers: One helper admitted with each fan with disabilities
Prices: Normal prices apply
Disabled Toilets: Available
Contact: (01253) 599344 (Bookings are necessary)

Travelling Supporters' Information: From All Parts: Exit M6 at Junction 32 onto the M55. Follow signs for the main car parks along the new 'spine' road to the car parks at the side of the ground.

BOLTON WANDERERS FC

Founded: 1874 (**Entered League**: 1888)
Former Names: Christchurch FC (1874-1877)
Nickname: 'Trotters'
Ground: Toughsheet Community Stadium,
Burnden Way, Lostock, Bolton   BL6 6JW
Ground Capacity: 28,723 (All seats)
Record Attendance: 28,353 (vs Leicester City, 2003)

Colours: White shirts with Navy Blue shorts
Telephone Nº: (01204) 673673
Ticket Office: (01204) 328888
Website: www.bwfc.co.uk
E-mail: reception@bwfc.co.uk

GENERAL INFORMATION

Car Parking: 2,800 spaces available at the ground (£7.00)
Coach Parking: Available at the ground (£20.00)
Nearest Railway Station: Horwich Parkway (600 yards)
Nearest Bus Station: Moor Lane, Bolton
Club Shop: At the ground
Opening Times: Daily from 9.30am to 5.30pm
Telephone Nº: (01204) 673650

GROUND INFORMATION

Away Supporters' Entrances & Sections:
South Stand entrances and accommodation

ADMISSION INFO (2024/2025 PRICES)

Adult Seating: From £28.00
Concessionary Seating: From £23.00
Under-18s Seating: From £17.00
Under-12s Seating: From £12.00
Note: Prices vary depending on the grading of the game.

FANS WITH DISABILITIES INFORMATION

Wheelchairs: 32 spaces available for visiting fans, 72 spaces for home fans
Helpers: One helper admitted free with each disabled fan
Prices: Normal prices apply for fans with disabilities
Disabled Toilets: Available
Contact: (01204) 328888   (Bookings are necessary)
Daniel Scott (DLO) – dscott@bwfc.co.uk

Travelling Supporters' Information:
From All Parts: Exit the M61 at Junction 6 and the ground is clearly visible ¼ mile away.

BRISTOL ROVERS FC

Founded: 1883 (**Re-entered League**: 2015)
Former Names: Black Arabs FC (1883-84);
Eastville Rovers FC (1884-96);
Bristol Eastville Rovers FC (1896-97)
Nickname: 'Pirates' 'Rovers' 'Gas'
Ground: The Memorial Stadium, Filton Avenue,
Horfield, Bristol BS7 0BF

Ground Capacity: 11,000
Seating Capacity: 3,307
Record Attendance: 12,011 (9th March 2008)
Colours: Blue & White quartered shirts, White shorts
Telephone N°: (0117) 909-6648
Website: www.bristolrovers.co.uk

GENERAL INFORMATION
Car Parking: Very limited number of spaces at the ground
and street parking
Coach Parking: At the ground
Nearest Railway Station: Temple Meads (2 miles)
Nearest Bus Station: Bristol City Centre
Club Shop: At the ground
Opening Times: Monday to Friday, 9.00am to 5.00pm.
Open from 9.00am to 1.00pm on non-match Saturdays and
9.00am until kick-off then after the game on matchdays.
Telephone N°: (0117) 909-6648 Option 1

GROUND INFORMATION
Away Supporters' Entrances & Sections:
Entrance to East Terrace & South Stand via Filton Avenue

ADMISSION INFO (2024/2025 PRICES)
Adult Standing: £15.00 – £25.00
Adult Seating: £25.00 – £35.00
Under-21s/ Concessionary Standing: £10.00 – £20.00
Under-21s/Concessionary Seating: £20.00 – £30.00
Under-14s Standing: £5.00 – £10.00
Under-14s Seating: £5.00 – £20.00

FANS WITH DISABILITIES INFORMATION
Wheelchairs: 38 spaces in total including 10 spaces for
Away fans in front of the East Stand and West Stand
Helpers: One helper admitted per fan with disabilities
Prices: Normal prices (depending on age) for disabled fans.
Helpers are admitted free
Disabled Toilets: Available in the East Stand and West Stand
Contact: (0117) 909-6648 Option 1 (Bookings are necessary)

Travelling Supporters' Information: Routes: From All Parts: Exit the M32 at Junction 2 then take the exit at the roundabout
(signposted Horfield) into Muller Road. Continue for approximately 1½ miles passing straight across 3 sets of traffic lights. At the
6th set of traffic lights turn left into Filton Avenue and the ground is immediately on the left.

BURTON ALBION FC

Founded: 1950 (**Entered League**: 2009)
Former Names: None
Nickname: 'The Brewers'
Ground: The Pirelli Stadium, Princess Way,
Burton-on-Trent   DE13 0AR
Ground Capacity: 6,912 **Seating Capacity**: 2,034

Record Attendance: 6,746 (vs Derby County, 2016)
Colours: Yellow shirts with Black trim, Black shorts
Telephone Nº: (01283) 565938
Website: www.burtonalbionfc.co.uk
E-mail: bafc@burtonalbionfc.co.uk

GENERAL INFORMATION

Car Parking: 400 spaces available at the ground (£5.00)
Coach Parking: Available at Claymills Pumping Station, Meadow Lane, Burton-on-Trent DE13 0DA (approximately 1 mile). Stewards will direct if necessary.
Nearest Railway Station: Burton-on-Trent (1½ miles)
Nearest Bus Station: Burton-on-Trent (1½ miles)
Club Shop: At the ground
Opening Times: Weekdays 8.30am to 5.30pm and Saturday Matchdays from 9.00am until 5.30pm (but only until noon on non-matchdays)
Telephone Nº: (01283) 565938

GROUND INFORMATION

Away Supporters' Entrances & Sections:
Main Stand and East Terrace

ADMISSION INFO (2024/2025 PRICES)

Adult Standing: £20.00   **Adult Seating**: £24.00
Under-17s Standing: £7.00   **Under-17s Seating**: £14.00
Ages 17 to 22 Standing: £15.00   **Seating**: £22.00
Senior Citizen Standing: £18.00   **Seating**: £22.00
Note: Cheaper 'Early bird' prices are available for tickets purchased before 5.00pm on the day before the game.

FANS WITH DISABILITIES INFORMATION

Wheelchairs: Over 60 spaces available for home and away fans in designated areas (East Terrace for away fans).
Helpers: Admitted
Prices: Normal prices for fans with disabilities. Helpers free
Disabled Toilets: Available in all stands
Contact: (01283) 565938   (Bookings are necessary)

Travelling Supporters' Information:
Routes: From the M1, North and South: Exit at Junction 23A and join the A50 towards Derby (also signposted for Alton Towers). Join the A38 southbound at the Toyota factory (towards Burton & Lichfield) then exit for Burton North onto the A5121. Continue past the Pirelli factory on the right and the BP Garage and Cash & Carry on the left then turn into Princess Way at the roundabout; From the M5/6 South: Join the M42 northbound and exit onto the A446 signposted Lichfield. Follow signs for the A38 to Burton then exit onto A5121 as above; From the M6 North: Exit at Junction 15 and follow the A50 towards Stoke and Uttoxeter. Exit the A50 for the A38 southbound signposted Burton and Lichfield at the Toyota factory, then as above. SatNav users should enter the following post code: DE13 0BH

CAMBRIDGE UNITED FC

Founded: 1912   (**Re-entered League**: 2014)
Former Name: Abbey United FC (1912-1951)
Nickname: 'U's' 'United'
Ground: Abbey Stadium, Newmarket Road, Cambridge   CB5 8LN
Ground Capacity: 8,127
Seating Capacity: 4,376

Record Attendance: 14,000 (1st May 1970)
Colours: Amber and Black striped shirts, Black shorts
Telephone Nº: (01223) 566500
Ticket Office: (01223) 566500 (Option 1)
Website: www.cambridgeunited.com
E-mail: info@cambridgeunited.com

GENERAL INFORMATION

Car Parking: Street parking or use Park and Ride
Coach Parking: Coldhams Road
Nearest Railway Station: Cambridge (2 miles)
Nearest Bus Station: Cambridge City Centre
Club Shop: At the ground
Opening Times: Monday to Friday 10.00am to 4.00pm and Matchdays 10.00am to kick-off
Telephone Nº: (01223) 566500 Option 2

GROUND INFORMATION

Away Supporters' Entrances & Sections:
Coldham Common turnstiles 20-22 – Habbin Terrace (South) and South Stand (Seating) turnstiles 23-26

ADMISSION INFO (2024/2025 PRICES)

Adult Standing: £23.00   **Seating**: £25.00 – £29.00
Concessionary Standing: £21.00
Concessionary Seating: £21.00 – £25.00
Under-18s Standing/Seating: £14.00 – £22.00
Under-14s Standing/Seating: £9.00 – £11.00

FANS WITH DISABILITIES INFORMATION

Wheelchairs: 35 spaces for Home fans in sections in front of Main Stand and in the North Terrace. 10 spaces for Away fans in the South Stand.
Helpers: One helper admitted per fan with disabilities
Prices: Normal prices apply for the disabled. Free for helpers
Disabled Toilets: Available
Contact: (01223) 566500 Option 8 (Early booking strongly advised) – davem@cambridgeunited.com

Travelling Supporters' Information: From the North: Take the A14 from Huntingdon, then turn east along the A14 dual carriageway. Exit the A14 at the 4th junction (to the east of Cambridge), up the slip road signposted Stow-cum-Quy then turn right onto the A1303, returning westwards towards Cambridge. Go straight on at the first roundabout passing the Airport on the left then straight on at two sets of traffic lights. Go straight on at the next roundabout and the ground is on the left after 700 yards; From the South: Exit the M11 at Junction 14 and turn east along the A14 dual carriageway. Then as from the North.
Bus Services: Services from the Railway Station to the City Centre and Nº 3 from the City Centre to the Ground.

CHARLTON ATHLETIC FC

Founded: 1905 (**Entered League**: 1921)
Nickname: 'Addicks'
Ground: The Valley, Floyd Road, Charlton, London, SE7 8BL
Ground Capacity: 27,111 (All seats)
Record Attendance: 75,031 (12th February 1938)

Colours: Red shirts with White shorts
Telephone Nº: (020) 8333-4000
Ticket Office: 03330 144444
Website: www.charltonafc.com
E-mail: info@charltonafc.com

GENERAL INFORMATION

Car Parking: Street Parking
Coach Parking: By Police direction
Nearest Railway Station: Charlton (2 minutes walk)
Nearest Bus Station: At Charlton Railway Station as above
Club Shop: At the ground
Opening Times: Tuesday to Saturday 10.00am to 3.00pm
Telephone Nº: (020) 8333-4035

GROUND INFORMATION

Away Supporters' Entrances & Sections:
Valley Grove/Jimmy Seed Stand

ADMISSION INFO (2024/2025 PRICES)

Adult Seating: £24.00 – £30.00
Senior Citizen/Under-21s Seating: £22.00 – £23.00
Under-18s Seating: £14.00 – £15.00
Under-11s Seating: £6.00

FANS WITH DISABILITIES INFORMATION

Wheelchairs: 96 spaces available for Home fans around the ground. 7 spaces available for Away fans in the South (Jimmy Seed) Stand
Helpers: One helper admitted per fan with disabilities
Prices: Normal prices for disabled fans. Helpers free
Disabled Toilets: Available in West and East Stands
Commentaries are available – please ring for details
Contact: 03330 144444 (Ticket Office –Bookings are necessary) or contact (020) 8333-4000.

Travelling Supporters' Information:
Routes: From All Parts: Exit the M25 at Junction 2 (A2 London-bound) and follow until the road becomes the A102(M). Take the exit marked Woolwich Ferry and turn right along the A206 Woolwich Road. After approximately 1 mile do a U-turn at the roundabout back along Woolwich Road. At the traffic lights turn left into Charlton Church Lane and Floyd Road is the 2nd left.

CRAWLEY TOWN FC

Founded: 1896 (**Entered League**: 2011)
Former Names: None
Nickname: 'Red Devils'
Ground: The People's Pension Stadium, Winfield Way, Crawley, West Sussex RH11 9RX
Record Attendance: 5,880 (2013)

Colours: Red shirts and shorts
Telephone Nº: (01293) 410000 (Ground)
Ticket Office: (01293) 410000
Ground Capacity: 6,134
Seating Capacity: 3,295
Website: www.crawleytownfc.com
E-mail: feedback@crawleytownfc.com

GENERAL INFORMATION

Car Parking: Free parking is available in William Reed car park at Broadfield Park (5 minutes walk).
Coach Parking: At the ground
Nearest Railway Station: Crawley (1 mile)
Nearest Bus Station: By the Railway Station
Club Shop: At the ground
Opening Times: Weekdays 10.00am to 4.30pm (closed on Wednesdays) and Saturday matchdays from 10.00am onwards. Mid-week matches also open from 6.00pm to kick-off then for 30 minutes after the game.
Telephone Nº: (01293) 410000

GROUND INFORMATION

Away Supporters' Entrances & Sections:
North Entrance for terrace and seating in the KR-L Stand

ADMISSION INFO (2024/2025 PRICES)

Adult Standing: £18.00
Adult Seating: £20.00
Senior Citizen Standing: £13.00
Senior Citizen Seating: £15.00
Under-21s Standing: £8.00
Under-21s Seating: £8.00
Ages 14 to 16 Standing/Seating: £7.00
Under-14s Standing/Seating: Free with paying adult

FANS WITH DISABILITIES INFORMATION

Wheelchairs: Accommodated in the East or West Stands for home fans and the East Stand for away fans
Helpers: One helper admitted per fan with disabilities
Prices: Prices are dependant on levels of DLA received Free of charge for helpers
Disabled Toilets: Available around the ground
Contact: (01293) 530314 (Barb) (Bookings are necessary)

Travelling Supporters' Information:
Routes: Exit the M23 at Junction 11 and take the A23 towards Crawley. After ¼ mile, the Stadium is on the left. Take the first exit at the roundabout for the Stadium entrance.

EXETER CITY FC

Founded: 1901   (**Re-Entered League**: 2008)
Former Names: Formed by the amalgamation of St. Sidwell United FC & Exeter United FC
Nickname: 'The Grecians'
Ground: St. James Park, Exeter, EX4 6PX
Ground Capacity: 8,696
Seating Capacity: 3,600

Record Attendance: 21,013 (4th March 1931)
Colours: Red and White striped shirts, Black shorts
Telephone Nº: (01392) 411243
Ticket Office: (01392) 413952
Website: www.exetercityfc.co.uk
E-mail: reception@ecfc.co.uk

GENERAL INFORMATION

Car Parking: Parr Street, John Lewis and Bampfyled Street car parks
Coach Parking: Paris Street Bus Station (10 minute walk)
Nearest Railway Station: Exeter St. James Park (adjacent)
Nearest Bus Station: Paris Street Bus Station
Club Shop: At the ground
Opening Times: Monday to Friday 8.30am to 5.00pm and 11.00am to 5.30pm on matchdays.
Club Shop Telephone Nº: (01392) 411243 Option 3

GROUND INFORMATION

Away Supporters' Entrances & Sections:
St. James Road turnstiles for standing in the Marsh Kia St. James Road Stand or Blocks L and M of the IP Office Main Stand for seating.
Note: Cash is only taken on the Thatcher Gold Big Bank turnstiles. Away section tickets are sold at the booth adjacent to the St. James Road turnstiles.

ADMISSION INFO (2024/2025 PRICES)

Adult Standing: £22.00
Adult Seating: £29.00
Concessionary Standing: £19.00
Concessionary Seating: £26.00
Under-18s Standing: £10.00
Under-18s Seating: £15.00

FANS WITH DISABILITIES INFORMATION

Wheelchairs: Accommodated in the IP Office Main Stand, Stagecoach Stand and the Big Bank.
Helpers: One assistant admitted per wheelchair
Prices: Free of charge for assistants. Normal prices for fans with disabilities in the wheelchair area.
Disabled Toilets: Available by the Big Bank Stand
Contact: (01392) 411243   (Bookings are necessary) – Kay Crawford (DLO)   disability@exetercityfc.co.uk

Travelling Supporters' Information:
Routes: From the North: Exit the M5 at Junction 29 and follow signs to the City Centre along Heavitree Road. Take the 4th exit at the roundabout into Western Way and the 2nd exit into Tiverton Road then 2nd left into Stadium Way; From the East: Take the A30 into Heavitree Road (then as from the North); From the South & West: Take the A38 and follow City Centre signs into Western Way, then take the third exit at the roundabout into St. James Road.   (Follow the brown football signs from the M5)
Note: This ground is difficult to find being in a residential area on the side of a hill without prominent floodlights!

HUDDERSFIELD TOWN FC

Founded: 1908 (**Entered League**: 1910)
Nickname: 'Terriers'
Ground: The John Smith's Stadium, Stadium Way, Huddersfield HD1 6PX
Ground Capacity: 24,554 (All seats)
Record Attendance: 24,169 (30th September 2017)

Colours: Blue and White striped shirts, White shorts and socks
Telephone Nº: (01484) 960600
Ticket Office: (01484) 960606
Website: www.htafc.com
E-mail: info@htafc.com

GENERAL INFORMATION

Car Parking: No spaces available at the ground but private car parks on Leeds Road and St. Andrew's Road (not associated with the club) charge around £6.00 to park.
Coach Parking: Adjacent car park
Nearest Railway Station: Huddersfield (1¼ miles)
Nearest Bus Station: Huddersfield
Club Shop: At the ground and in the Packhorse Shopping Centre in King Street, Huddersfield
Opening Times: At the ground: Monday to Saturday 9.00am to 5.00pm, Saturday Matchdays 9.00am to 3.00pm. Packhorse Centre: Monday to Saturday 9.00am to 5.00pm
Telephone Nº: (01484) 960636 or (01484) 430192

GROUND INFORMATION

Away Supporters' Entrances & Sections:
Adzorb South Stand

ADMISSION INFO (2024/2025 PRICES)

Adult Seating: £25.00
Concessionary Seating: £20.00
Ages 12 to 18 Seating: £15.00
Under-12s Seating: £10.00
Note: Prices shown are for tickets purchased in advance.

FANS WITH DISABILITIES INFORMATION

Wheelchairs: 177 spaces in total for home and away fans in the special sections in the Adzorb South Stand, Revell Ward Stand and Britannia Rescue Stand. Additional spaces are available for the ambulant and visually impaired.
Helpers: Admitted
Prices: £15.00 – £25.00 for fans with disabilities. Helpers free
Disabled Toilets: Available in the each of the sections Commentaries are available for the blind.
Contact: (01484) 960606 Option 5 (Bookings necessary) dlo@htafc.com

Travelling Supporters' Information:
Routes: From the North, East and West: Exit the M62 at Junction 25 and take the A644 and A62 following Huddersfield signs. Follow signs for the Galpharm Stadium; From the South: Leave the M1 at Junction 38 and follow the A637/A642 to Huddersfield. At the Ring Road, follow signs for the A62 to the Galpharm Stadium.

LEYTON ORIENT FC

Founded: 1881   (**Re-entered League**: 2019)
Former Names: Glyn Cricket and Football Club
(1881-86); Eagle FC (1886-88); Clapton Orient FC
(1888-1946); Leyton Orient FC (1946-66); Orient FC
(1966-87)
Nickname: 'O's'
Ground: Gaughan Group Stadium, Brisbane Road,
Oliver Road, Leyton, London   E10 5NF

Ground Capacity: 9,271 (all seats)
Record Attendance: 34,345 (21st January 1964)
Telephone N°: (020) 8926-1111
Ticket Office: (020) 8926-1010
Website: www.leytonorient.com
E-mail: enquiries@leytonorient.net

GENERAL INFORMATION
Car Parking: Street parking
Coach Parking: By Police direction
Nearest Railway Station: Leyton Midland Road (½ mile)
Nearest Tube Station: Leyton (Central)
Club Shop: At the ground
Opening Times: Weekdays and Home Matchdays 10.00am
to 3.00pm
Telephone N°: (020) 8926-1111

GROUND INFORMATION
Away Supporters' Entrances & Sections:
East Stand

ADMISSION INFO (2024/2026 PRICES)
Adult Seating: £27.00 – £55.00
Senior Citizen/Concessionary Seating: £25.00 – £45.00
Under-18s Seating: £11.00 – £45.00
Under-11s Seating: £6.00 – £11.00
Note: Tickets are cheaper when purchased in advance

FANS WITH DISABILITIES INFORMATION
Wheelchairs: Spaces are available in the North, East and
West Stands
Helpers: One helper admitted per fan with disabilities
Prices: Normal prices for fans with disabilities. Helpers free
Disabled Toilets: Available near the disabled sections
Contact: (020) 8926-1111 (Bookings are
necessary) Lindsay Martin (DLO) l.martin@leytonorient.net

Travelling Supporters' Information:
Routes: From the North & West: Take A406 North Circular, follow signs for Chelmsford to Edmonton. After 2½ miles take the
3rd exit at the roundabout towards Leyton (A112). Pass the railway station, turn right after ½ mile into Windsor Road and left
into Brisbane Road; From the East: Follow the A12 to London then the City for Leytonstone. Follow Hackney signs into Grove
Road, cross Main Road into Ruckholt Road then turn right into Leyton High Road, turn left after ¼ mile into Buckingham Road
and left into Brisbane Road; From the South: Take the A102M through the Blackwall Tunnel, follow signs for Newmarket (A102)
to join the A11 to Stratford, then follow signs for Stratford Station into Leyton Road to the railway station (then as from North).

LINCOLN CITY FC

Founded: 1884 (**Re-entered League**: 2017)
Nickname: 'Red Imps'
Ground: LNER Stadium, Lincoln   LN5 8LD
Ground Capacity: 10,120 (All seats)
Record Attendance: 23,196 (15th November 1967)

Colours: Red and White striped shirts, Black shorts
Telephone N°: (01522) 880011
Ticket Office: (01522) 880011
Website: www.weareimps.com
E-mail: admin@theredimps.com

GENERAL INFORMATION

Car Parking: No specific parking for visiting fans.
Street parking or the City Centre car parks are the only option.
Coach Parking: Please contact the club for details.
Nearest Railway Station: Lincoln Central
Club Shop: At the ground and at Waterside in Lincoln
Opening Times: Monday to Saturday 10.00am to 4.00pm and Saturday Matchdays 10.00am until kick-off and then after the final whistle until 5.30pm. Open from 10.00am until kick-off on midweek matchdays.
Telephone N°: (01522) 539399 or (01522) 690674

GROUND INFORMATION

Away Supporters' Entrances & Sections:
Stacey West Stand – Turnstiles 4 to 8

ADMISSION INFO (2024/2025 PRICES)

Adult Seating: £27.00
Concessionary Seating: £22.00
Under-18s Seating: £14.00
Under-14s Seating: £10.00
Note: Discounts are available for members.

FANS WITH DISABILITIES INFORMATION

Wheelchairs: 37 spaces available for home fans and 6 spaces available for away fans in a special section
Helpers: One helper admitted per fan with disabilities
Prices: Helpers are admitted free of charge if the supporter they are assisting is in receipt of the higher rate of disability allowance or enhanced PIP.
Disabled Toilets: 5 available in total
Contact: (01522) 880011 (Bookings are necessary)
dlo@theredimps.com

Travelling Supporters' Information:
Routes: From the East: Take the A46 or A158 into the City Centre following Newark (A46) signs into the High Street and take next left (Scorer Street and Cross Street) for the ground; From the North and West: Take the A15 or A57 into the City Centre, then as from the East; From the South: Take the A1 then A46 for the City Centre, then into the High Street, parking on the South Common or in the Stadium via South Park Avenue, turn down by the Fire Station.

MANSFIELD TOWN FC

Founded: 1897 (**Re-entered League**: 1892)
Former Name: Mansfield Wesleyans FC (1897-1905)
Nickname: 'Stags'
Ground: One Call Stadium, Quarry Lane, Mansfield, Nottinghamshire   NG18 5DA
Ground Capacity: 9,376 (All seats)
Record Attendance: 24,467 (10th January 1953)

Colours: Amber shirts with Royal Blue piping, Royal Blue shorts with Amber flash
Telephone Nº: (01623) 482482
Ticket Office: (01623) 482482
Website: www.mansfieldtown.net
E-mail: info@mansfieldtown.net

GENERAL INFORMATION

Car Parking: Small car park at the ground (£5.00)
Coach Parking: Adjacent to the ground
Nearest Railway Station: Mansfield (5 minutes walk)
Nearest Bus Station: Mansfield
Club Shop: In the South Stand of the Stadium
Opening Times: Weekdays 10.00am – 5.00pm and Matchdays 10.00am – 3.00pm
Telephone Nº: (01623) 482482

GROUND INFORMATION

Away Supporters' Entrances & Sections:
North Stand turnstiles for North Stand seating

ADMISSION INFO (2024/2025 PRICES)

Adult Seating: £23.00 – £25.00
Senior Citizen Seating: £21.00 – £22.00
Ages 18 to 21 Seating: £19.00 – £20.00
Ages 13 to 17 Seating: £15.00 – £16.00
Ages 7 to 12 Seating: £11.00 – £12.00
Under-7s Seating: Free of charge

FANS WITH DISABILITIES INFORMATION

Wheelchairs: 90 spaces available in total in special sections in the North Stand, Quarry Street Stand and West Stand
Helpers: Admitted
Prices: Normal prices apply for the disabled. Free for helpers
Disabled Toilets: Available in the North Stand, West Stand and Quarry Lane Stand
Contact: (01623) 482482 (Please buy tickets in advance)
Alan Lakin (DLO) – safetyofficer@mansfieldtown.net

Travelling Supporters' Information:
Routes: From the North: Exit the M1 at Junction 29 and take the A617 to Mansfield. After 6¼ miles turn right at the Leisure Centre into Rosemary Street. Carry on to Quarry Lane and turn right; From the South and West: Exit the M1 at Junction 28 and take the A38 to Mansfield. After 6½ miles turn right at the crossroads into Belvedere Street then turn right after ¼ mile into Quarry Lane; From the East: Take the A617 to Rainworth, turn left at the crossroads after 3 miles into Windsor Road and turn right at the end into Nottingham Road, then left into Quarry Lane.

NORTHAMPTON TOWN FC

Founded: 1897 (**Entered League**: 1920)
Nickname: 'Cobblers'
Ground: Sixfields Stadium, Upton Way, Northampton NN5 5QA
Ground Capacity: 7,798 (All seats)
Record Attendance: 7,798 (September 2016)

Colours: Claret and White shirts with White shorts
Telephone Nº: (01604) 683700
Ticket Office: (01604) 683777
Website: www.ntfc.co.uk
E-mail: wendy.lambell@ntfc.co.uk

GENERAL INFORMATION

Car Parking: At the ground
Coach Parking: At the ground
Nearest Railway Station: Northampton Castle (2 miles)
Nearest Bus Station: North Gate
Club Shop: At the ground
Opening Times: Monday to Friday 9.00am – 5.00pm..
Saturday Matchdays 11.00am to 5.00pm and non-match
Saturdays 9.00am to 12.00pm.
Telephone Nº: (01604) 683777

GROUND INFORMATION

Away Supporters' Entrances & Sections:
Moulton College Stand

ADMISSION INFO (2024/2025 PRICES)

Adult Seating: £26.00
Senior Citizen Seating: £22.00
Under-21s Seating: £22.00
Under-18s Seating: £14.00
Under-14s Seating: £10.00
Under-7s: Admitted free of charge
Note: Discounted prices are available for advance purchases

FANS WITH DISABILITIES INFORMATION

Wheelchairs: 55 spaces in total for Home and Away fans in various areas of the ground
Helpers: One helper admitted per fan with disabilities
Prices: Normal prices for fans with disabilities. Helpers free
Disabled Toilets: Available
Commentaries are available for the blind
Contact: (01604) 683777   (Bookings are necessary) –
wendy.lambell@ntfc.co.uk (Supporters' Liaison Officer) –
07714 407448

Travelling Supporters' Information:
Routes: From All Parts: Exit the M1 at Junction 15A following the signs for Sixfields Leisure onto Upton Way – the ground is approximately 2 miles.

PETERBOROUGH UNITED FC

Founded: 1934 (**Entered League**: 1960)
Nickname: 'Posh'
Ground: The Weston Homes Stadium, London Road, Peterborough PE2 8AL
Ground Capacity: 15,314 (All Seats)
Record Attendance: 30,096 (20th February 1965)

Colours: Cobalt Blue shirts with Blue shorts
Telephone Nº: (01733) 563947
Ticket Office: (01733) 865674
Website: www.theposh.com
E-mail: info@theposh.com

GENERAL INFORMATION

Car Parking: Adjacent to the ground at the Pleasure Fair Meadow council car park and the Railworld car park.
Coach Parking: In front of the (North) Main Stand
Nearest Railway Station: Peterborough (1 mile)
Nearest Bus Station: Peterborough (1 mile)
Club Shop: At the ground
Opening Times: Tuesday to Friday 9.00am to 5.00pm (from 10.00am on Mondays). Saturday Matchdays 10.00pm to 3.00pm then 5.00pm to 5.30pm
Telephone Nº: (01733) 865668

GROUND INFORMATION

Away Supporters' Entrances & Sections:
Blocks 'A' and 'B' of the North Stand

ADMISSION INFO (2024/2025 PRICES)

Adult Seating: £26.00 – £30.00
Senior Citizen Seating: £21.00 – £25.00
Ages 18 to 23 Seating: £17.00 – £21.00
Ages 14 to 17 Seating: £11.00
Under-14s Seating: £3.00 – £5.00
Note: Discounts are available for tickets purchased in advance

FANS WITH DISABILITIES INFORMATION

Wheelchairs: 57 spaces available in total in the South Stand, North Stand and Motorpoint Stand
Helpers: One helper admitted per fan with disabilities
Prices: Normal prices for fans with disabilities. Helpers free
Disabled Toilets: Available in all areas of the ground
Contact: (01733) 865674 Option 2 (Bookings are necessary) Chris Abbott – fans@theposh.com

Travelling Supporters' Information:
Routes: From the North and West: Take the A1 then the A47 into the Town Centre and follow Whittlesey signs across the river into London Road; From the East: Take the A47 into the Town Centre (then as from the North); From the South: Take the A1 then the A15 into London Road.

READING FC

Founded: 1871 (**Entered League**: 1920)
Former Names: Formed by the amalgamation of Hornets FC (1877) and Earley FC (1889)
Nickname: 'Royals'
Ground: Select Car Leasing Stadium, Junction 11 M4, Reading, Berkshire RG2 0FL
Ground Capacity: 24,161 (All seats)

Record Attendance: 24,184 (vs Everton, 17/11/12)
Colours: Blue and White hooped shirts, White shorts
Telephone Nº: (0118) 968-1100
Ticket Office: (0118) 968-1313
Website: www.readingfc.co.uk
E-mail: supporterservices@readingfc.co.uk

GENERAL INFORMATION

Car Parking: 1,800 spaces available at the ground (£10.00). Also another 2,000 spaces available nearby
Coach Parking: Please contact the club for details
Nearest Railway Station: Reading Central
Nearest Bus Station: Reading
Club Shop: At the ground
Opening Times: Monday to Saturday 9.00am – 5.30pm
Telephone Nº: (0118) 968-1234

GROUND INFORMATION

Away Supporters' Entrances & Sections:
Turnstiles 9 and 10 for South Stand accommodation

ADMISSION INFO (2024/2025 PRICES)

Adult Seating: £23.00 – £30.00
Over-65s Seating: £20.00 – £23.00
Ages 18 to 24 Seating: £17.00 – £20.00
Ages 14 to 17 Seating: £12.00 – £15.00
Under-14s Seating: £5.00 – £11.00
Note: Prices shown are for matchday ticket purchases.
Discounts are available to members and for advance purchases

FANS WITH DISABILITIES INFORMATION

Wheelchairs: 73 spaces are available for home fans and 14 spaces are available for away fans throughout the stadium
Prices: Normal prices apply for fans with disabilities. Helpers are admitted free of charge
Disabled Toilets: Available
Commentaries for approximately 12 people are available
Contact: (0118) 968-1313 Option 2 (Bookings necessary) disability@readingfc.co.uk

Travelling Supporters' Information:
Routes: The stadium is situated just off Junction 11 of the M4 near Reading.

ROTHERHAM UNITED FC

Founded: 1870 (**Entered League**: 1893)
Former Names: Rotherham Town FC (1870-1896), Thornhill United FC (1884-1905) and Rotherham County FC (1905-1925)
Nickname: 'The Millers'
Ground: The AESSEAL New York Stadium, New York Way, Rotherham S60 1AH
Ground Capacity: 12,000 (All seats)

Record Attendance: 11,758 (7th September 2013)
Colours: Red shirts with White sleeves, White shorts
Telephone Nº: (01709) 827760
Ticket Office: (01709) 827768
Website: www.themillers.co.uk
E-mail: office@rotherhamunited.net

GENERAL INFORMATION

Car Parking: Street Parking and in Sheffield Road car parks
Coach Parking: At the stadium by arrangement (£25.00)
Nearest Railway Station: Rotherham Central (½ mile)
Nearest Bus Station: Rotherham Town Centre (½ mile)
Club Shop: At the ground
Opening Times: Weekdays 9.00am to 5.00pm, Saturdays 9.00am to 1.00pm (Matchdays until 30 minutes after kick-off)
Telephone Nº: (01709) 827768

GROUND INFORMATION

Away Supporters' Entrances & Sections:
Meditemp Stand

ADMISSION INFO (2024/2025 PRICES)

Adult Seating: £27.00 – £31.00
Senior Citizen/Student Seating: £20.00 – £24.00
Ages 13 to 17 Seating: £10.00 – £13.00
Under-13s Seating: £9.00 – £11.00
Under-8s Seating: £4.00 in the Family Stand

FANS WITH DISABILITIES INFORMATION

Wheelchairs: Accommodated
Helpers: One helper admitted with each fan with disabilities
Prices: Supporters with disabilities are charged concessionary prices. Helpers are admitted free of charge
Disabled Toilets: Available
Contact: (01709) 827768 (Bookings are necessary)
Cameron Harris (DLO) – dlo@rotherhamunited.net

Travelling Supporters' Information:
Routes: From the North: Exit the M1 at Junction 34, follow Rotherham (A6109) signs to the traffic lights and turn right. The ground is ¼ mile on the right; From the South & West: Exit the M1 at Junction 33, turn right and follow signs for Rotherham. Turn left at the roundabout then right at the next roundabout. Follow the dual carriageway and continue straight on at the next roundabout. Turn left at the following roundabout and the ground is on the left after ¼ mile; From the East: Take the A630 into Rotherham following Sheffield signs. Turn left at the 3rd roundabout (signposted Masborough) and the ground is on the right.

SHREWSBURY TOWN FC

Founded: 1886 (**Entered League**: 1950)
Nickname: 'Salop' 'The Shrews' 'The Blues' 'Town'
Ground: The Croud Meadow, Oteley Road,
Shrewsbury SY2 6ST
Ground Capacity: 9,875 (All seats)
Record Attendance: 9,510 (September 2013)

Colours: Shirts and shorts are Blue and Amber
Telephone N°: (01743) 289177
Ticket Office: (01743) 273943
Website: www.shrewsburytown.com
E-mail: info@shrewsburytown.co.uk

GENERAL INFORMATION

Car Parking: Limited parking at the stadium – Permit
Holders only. Parking restrictions are imposed on matchdays
with no parking allowed in the vicinity of the stadium.
Visiting fans should use the Meole Brace Park & Ride Scheme
– £2.00 per person for the return journey – see details below
Coach Parking: At the stadium
Nearest Railway Station: Shrewsbury (2½ miles)
Nearest Bus Station: Raven Meadows, Shrewsbury
Club Shop: At the ground
Opening Times: Monday to Friday 9.00am to 5.00pm.
Saturday Matchdays 10.00am until kick-off.
Telephone N°: (01743) 289177

GROUND INFORMATION

Away Supporters' Entrances & Sections:
North Stand entrances and accommodation

ADMISSION INFO (2024/2025 PRICES)

Adult Seating: £25.00 – £28.00
Concessionary Seating: £18.00 – £20.00
Ages 19 to 23/Student Seating: £18.00 – £20.00
Ages 14 to 18 Seating: £11.00
Under-14s Seating: £1.00 – £2.00
Note: Prices vary depending on the category of the game

FANS WITH DISABILITIES INFORMATION

Wheelchairs: 94 spaces for home fans and 20 spaces for
away fans in the North, South and East Stands
Helpers: One helper admitted per fan with disabilities
Prices: Concessionary prices for fans with disabilities.
Helpers are admitted free of charge
Disabled Toilets: 30 available throughout the ground
Contact: (01743) 289177   (Bookings are necessary)

Travelling Supporters' Information:
Park & Ride information: Buses run every 15 minutes from 12.30pm to 2.30pm on Saturday matchdays and 6.15pm to
7.30pm on matchdays in the week. Parking is free and the return bus journey is £2.00 per person. Buses return to the car parks
immediately after the match finishes and car parks will remain open for one hour only. Car Park Locations:
Oxon Park and Ride Site: From the West and North West. At the junction of the A5 and the A458 (Churncote Roundabout)
follow the signs A458 'Shrewsbury Town Centre'. Oxon Park and Ride Site is clearly signposted; **The Shirehall**: From all routes
proceed along the A5 to Emstrey Island Roundabout into Shrewsbury, take the A5064 along London Road to the Column
roundabout. Take the 3rd exit at the roundabout and the first right into the Shirehall Car Park; **Shirehall Overflow Car Park**:
Follow directions to London Road as above. Before you reach the roundabout the car park is on the right-hand side. Proceed on
foot to the Shirehall main car park for the bus.

STEVENAGE FC

Founded: 1976
Former Names: None
Nickname: 'Boro'
Ground: Lamex Stadium, Broadhall Way, Stevenage, Hertfordshire   SG2 8RH
Record Attendance: 8,040 (25th January 1998)

Colours: Red and White shirts with Red shorts
Telephone Nº: (01438) 223223
Ground Capacity: 7,800
Seating Capacity: 3,404
Website: www.stevenagefc.com
E-mail: info@stevenagefc.com

GENERAL INFORMATION

Car Parking: Fairlands Show Ground (opposite)
Coach Parking: None at the Stadium
Nearest Railway Station: Stevenage (1 mile)
Nearest Bus Station: Stevenage
Club Shop: At the ground
Opening Times: Tuesday and Friday 10.00am to 5.00pm, Thursday 10.00am to 7.00pm, Tuesday and Saturday Matchdays from 12.00pm to kick-off then for 15 minutes after the game.
Telephone Nº: (01438) 223223

GROUND INFORMATION

Away Supporters' Entrances & Sections:
South Stand entrances and accommodation

ADMISSION INFO (2024/2025 PRICES)

Adult Standing: £22.00
Adult Seating: £25.00 – £26.00
Under-18s Standing: £15.00
Under-18s Seating: £17.00 – £19.00
Under-12s Standing: £5.00
Under-12s Seating: £10.00 – £12.00
Concessionary Standing: £20.00
Concessionary Seating: £24.00

FANS WITH DISABILITIES INFORMATION

Wheelchairs: 13 spaces available by the North Terrace
Helpers: Admitted
Prices: Concessionary prices apply for fans with disabilities. Free of charge for helpers
Disabled Toilets: Yes
Contact: (01438) 223223   (Bookings are necessary)
dslo@stevenagefc.com

Travelling Supporters' Information:
Routes: Exit the A1(M) at Junction 7 and take the B197. The ground is on the right at the 2nd roundabout.
Bus Routes: SB4 and SB5

STOCKPORT COUNTY FC

Photograph courtesy of Mike Petch – Mphotographic.co.uk

Founded: 1883
Former Names: Heaton Norris Rovers FC
Nickname: 'Hatters' 'County'
Ground: Edgeley Park, Hardcastle Road, Edgeley, Stockport SK3 9DD
Ground Capacity: 10,841 (All seats)
Record Attendance: 27,833 (11th February 1950)

Colours: Blue shirts and shorts
Telephone Nº: (0161) 266-2700
Ticket Office: (0161) 266-2700
Ticket Office E-mail: tickets@stockportcounty.com
Website: www.stockportcounty.com
E-mail: info@stockportcounty.com

GENERAL INFORMATION

Car Parking: Available at the end of Castle Street in Edgeley
Coach Parking: As above
Nearest Railway Station: Stockport (5 minutes walk)
Nearest Bus Station: Mersey Square (10 minutes walk)
Club Shop: At the ground
Opening Times: Wednesdays and Thursdays 12.00pm–4.00pm and Fridays 12.00pm to 6.00pm.
Telephone Nº: (0161) 266-2700

GROUND INFORMATION

Away Supporters' Entrances & Sections:
Viridor (Railway) End turnstiles and accommodation or turnstiles for Popular Side depending on the opponents

ADMISSION INFO (2024/2025 PRICES)

Adult Seating: £24.00
Concessionary Seating: £18.00
Ages 14 to 17 Seating: £11.00
Ages 6 to 13 Seating: £9.00
Note: Children under the age of 6 are admitted free when accompanied by a paying adult.

DISABLED INFORMATION

Wheelchairs: 16 spaces in total. 10 in the Hardcastle Road Stand, 6 in the Cheadle Stand
Helpers: One helper admitted per disabled fan
Prices: Concessionary prices for disabled fans. Helpers are admitted free of charge
Disabled Toilets: Available
Contact: (0161) 266-2700   (Bookings are necessary) – slo@stockportcounty.com

Travelling Supporters' Information:
Routes: From the North, South and West: Exit the M60 at Junction 1 and join the A560, following signs for Cheadle. After ¼ mile turn right into Edgeley Road and after 1 mile turn right into Caroline Street for the ground; From the East: Take the A6 or A560 into Stockport Town Centre and turn left into Greek Street. Take the 2nd exit into Mercian Way (from the roundabout) then turn left into Caroline Street – the ground is straight ahead.

WIGAN ATHLETIC FC

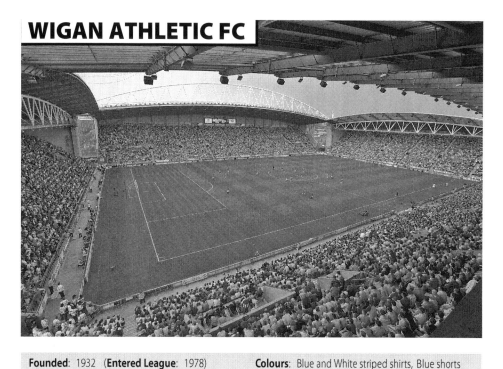

Founded: 1932 (**Entered League**: 1978)
Nickname: 'Latics'
Ground: The Brick Community Stadium, Loire Drive, Wigan, Lancashire WN5 0UZ
Ground Capacity: 25,146 (All seats)
Record Attendance: 25,133 (11th May 2008)

Colours: Blue and White striped shirts, Blue shorts
Telephone N°: (01942) 774000
Ticket Office: (01942) 311111
Website: www.wiganathletic.com
E-mail: feedback@wiganathletic.com

GENERAL INFORMATION

Car Parking: 2,000 spaces available at the ground (£5.00 for cars, £10.00 for minibuses, £20.00 for coaches)
Coach Parking: At the ground
Nearest Railway Station: Wallgate and Wigan North Western (1 mile)
Nearest Bus Station: Wigan
Club Shop: At the Stadium
Opening Times: Monday to Friday 10.00am to 5.00pm, Non-match Saturdays 10.00am to 4.00pm, Saturday Matchdays 10.00am to kick-off plus 30 minutes after the game
Telephone N°: (01942) 770450

GROUND INFORMATION

Away Supporters' Entrances & Sections: North Stand

ADMISSION INFO (2024/2025 PRICES)

Adult Seating: £23.00 – £28.00
Senior Citizen Seating: £18.00 – £22.00
18s to 21s Seating: £16.00 – £20.00
Under-18s Seating: £10.00
Under-12s Seating: £5.00
Under-5s Seating: £2.00

FANS WITH DISABILITIES INFORMATION

Wheelchairs: 206 spaces available in total
Helpers: One helper admitted with each fan with disabilities
Prices: Normal prices for fans with disabilities. Helpers free
Disabled Toilets: 20 available in total
Contact: (01942) 774000 (Bookings are necessary)

Travelling Supporters' Information:
Routes: From North: Exit M6 at Junction 27, turn left at end of slip road then right at T-junction, signposted Shevington. After 1 mile turn left at the mini-roundabout into Old Lane (B5375). After approx. 2 miles winding through countryside turn right at traffic lights into Scot Lane. Stadium is next left; From South & West: Exit M6 at Junction 25 follow signs for Wigan (A49). After approx. 2 miles a complex junction is reached, keep in left-hand lane (McDonalds on right). Turn left at traffic light filter lane into Robin Park Road. Turn right at third set of traffic lights and follow road to stadium; From East: Exit M61 Junction 6, take 1st exit at roundabout. At next roundabout take 1st left into Chorley Road. Follow signs for Wigan B5238, first turning right then left at Aspull Roundabout. After 2 miles turn right at traffic lights after Earl of Balcarres Pub to face Tesco. Turn left at lights, keep in left lane turn left at next lights with the Quality Hotel on the corner. Follow ring road, get into second lane from right as road bears right into Caroline Street, signposted Orrell. Continue on ring road as it bears left passing B&Q on left, pass Wigan Pier on right and as road goes under railway bridge get into right hand lane to turn right at lights into Robin Park Road. Then South & West.

WREXHAM AFC

Founded: 1864
Nickname: 'Red Dragons'
Ground: Racecourse Ground, Mold Road, Wrexham, North Wales LL11 2AH
Ground Capacity: 10,500 (all seats)
Record Attendance: 34,445 (26th January 1957)

Colours: Red shirts with White shorts
Telephone Nº: (01978) 891864
Website: www.wrexhamafc.co.uk
E-mail: info@wrexhamafc.co.uk

GENERAL INFORMATION

Car Parking: Town car parks are nearby and also Glyndwr University (Mold End)
Coach Parking: By Police direction
Nearest Railway Station: Wrexham General (adjacent)
Nearest Bus Station: Wrexham (King Street)
Club Shop: At the ground under the bkoncepts Stand
Opening Times: Monday to Friday 10.00am to 5.00pm and home Matchdays 10.00am until kick-off.
Telephone Nº: (01978) 891864

GROUND INFORMATION

Away Supporters' Entrances & Sections:
Turnstiles 1-4 for the bkoncepts Stand

ADMISSION INFO (2024/2025 PRICES)

Adult Seating: £19.00 – £22.00
Concession Seniors/Under-21s Seating: £14.00 – £17.00
Under-18s Seating: £7.00 – £10.00
Under-11s Seating: £5.00 (with a paying adult)
Note: Discounts apply for advance purchases and Family tickets are also available

DISABLED INFORMATION

Wheelchairs: 35 spaces in the Mold Road Stand
Helpers: One helper admitted per wheelchair
Prices: Normal prices for the disabled. Free for helpers
Disabled Toilets: Available in the disabled section
Contact: Kerry Evans (Disability Liaison Officer) – kerry.evans@wrexhamafc.co.uk

Travelling Supporters' Information:
Routes: From the North and West: Take the A483 and the Wrexham bypass to the junction with the A541. Branch left at the roundabout and follow Wrexham signs into Mold Road; From the East: Take the A525 or A534 into Wrexham then follow the A541 signs into Mold Road; From the South: Take the the M6, then the M54 and follow the A5 and A483 to the Wrexham bypass and the junction with the A541. Branch right at the roundabout and follow signs for the Town Centre.

WYCOMBE WANDERERS FC

Founded: 1887 (**Entered League**: 1993)
Nickname: 'The Blues' 'The Chairboys'
Ground: Adams Park, Hillbottom Road, Sands,
High Wycombe   HP12 4HJ
Ground Capacity: 9,448
Seating Capacity: 8,250

Record Attendance: 10,000 (vs Chelsea, July 2005)
Colours: Navy and Light Blue quarters with Navy shorts
Telephone Nº: (01494) 472100
Ticket Office: (01494) 441118
Website: www.wwfc.com
E-mail: wwfc@wwfc.com

GENERAL INFORMATION

Car Parking: Car park at the ground (£5.00) and also in Hillbottom Road
Coach Parking: Car park at the ground
Nearest Railway Station: High Wycombe
Nearest Bus Station: High Wycombe
Club Shop: At the ground
Opening Times: Monday to Friday 10.00am to 5.00pm but closed on Wednesdays. Also open from 10.00am on Saturday matchdays
Telephone Nº: (01494) 509510

GROUND INFORMATION

Away Supporters' Entrances & Sections:
Lords Builders Merchants Stand (seating only)

ADMISSION INFO (2024/2025 PRICES)

Adult Standing: £22.00   **Adult Seating**: £24.00–£31.00
Senior Citizen Standing: £19.00   **Seating**: £21 – £28
Ages 22-25 Standing: £18.00   **Seating**: £22.00–£26.00
Ages 19-21 Standing: £17.00   **Seating**: £18.00–£25.00
Ages 12-18 Standing: £9.00   **Seating**: £16.00–£20.00
Under-12s Seating: £5.00 – £15.00
Note: A £2.00 discount is available for advance purchases

FANS WITH DISABILITIES INFORMATION

Wheelchairs: 32 spaces in total available in special sections of the Family Stand and Away Stand
Helpers: One helper admitted per wheelchair
Prices: Full price for fans with disabilities. Free for helpers
Disabled Toilets: 4 available in the Family Stand
Commentaries are available for 5 people
Contact: (01494) 441118   (Bookings are necessary)

Travelling Supporters' Information:
Routes: From All Parts: Exit the M40 at Junction 4 and take the A4010 following Aylesbury signs. Go straight on at 3 mini-roundabouts then bear sharp left at the 4th roundabout into Lane End Road. Fork right into Hillbottom Road at the next roundabout. The ground is at the end of the road. Hillbottom Road is on the Sands Industrial Estate; From the Town Centre: Take the A40 West and after 1½ miles turn left into Chapel Lane (after the traffic lights). Turn right then right again at the mini-roundabout into Lane End Road – then as above.

EFL LEAGUE TWO

Website   www.efl.com
Email   info@efltrust.com

Clubs for the 2024/2025 Season

ACCRINGTON STANLEY FC

Founded: 1876 (Reformed 1968)
Former Names: None
Nickname: 'Stanley' 'Reds'
Ground: Wham Stadium, Livingstone Road, Accrington, Lancashire BB5 5BX
Record Attendance: 5,387 (26th January 2019)

Colours: Red shirts and shorts
Telephone N°: (01254) 356950
Ground Capacity: 5,450
Seating Capacity: 3,100
Website: www.accringtonstanley.co.uk
E-mail: info@accringtonstanley.co.uk

GENERAL INFORMATION

Car Parking: A limited number of spaces are available at the ground – pre-booking required with a £5.00 charge. Otherwise, street parking only.
Coach Parking: Livingstone Road near the Away entrance
Nearest Railway Station: Accrington (1 mile)
Nearest Bus Station: Accrington Town Centre (1 mile)
Club Shop: At the ground and through the club website
Opening Times: Weekdays 9.30am – 5.00pm; Saturday matchdays 10.30am – 5.30pm
Telephone N°: (01254) 356950

GROUND INFORMATION

Away Supporters' Entrances & Sections:
Coppice Terrace and in the Eric Wallace Stand

ADMISSION INFO (2024/2025 PRICES)

Adult Standing/Seating: £20.00 – £25.00
Senior Citizen Standing/Seating: £15.00 – £20.00
Ages 12-17 Standing/Seating: £10.00 – £15.00
Under-12s Standing/Seating: £5.00
Note: Prices depend on the category of the game.

FANS WITH DISABILITIES INFORMATION

Wheelchairs: Specific areas around the ground
Helpers: Admitted
Prices: Normal prices are charged for disabled fans. One helper is admitted free with each disabled supporter.
Disabled Toilets: Available
Contact: (01254) 356950 or 07754 665730 Robert Houseman, Liaison Officer (Bookings are necessary) – robert.houseman@accringtonstanley.co.uk

Travelling Supporters' Information:
Routes: Take the M6 to the M65 signposted for Blackburn/Burnley. Exit at Junction 7 and follow the sign for Padiham. Turn right at first traffic lights then right at next. Follow Whalley Road towards Accrington, go through lights at the Greyhound Inn. Turn left into Livingstone Road, 500 yards past traffic lights (signposted Accrington Stanley). The ground is signposted from Junction 7 of the M65 – follow the brown signs with the white football.

AFC WIMBLEDON

Founded: 2002 (**Entered League**: 2011)
Former Names: Originally formed as Wimbledon Old Centrals (1889-1905) who later became Wimbledon FC
Nickname: 'The Dons'
Ground: The Cherry Red Records Stadium, Plough Lane, Wimbledon   SW17 0NR

Record Attendance: 4,870 (2016 – King's Meadow)
Ground Capacity: 9,300 (All seats)
Colours: Shirts and Shorts are Blue with Yellow trim
Telephone Nº: (020) 8547-3528
Website: www.afcwimbledon.co.uk
E-mail: enquiries@afcwimbledon.co.uk

GENERAL INFORMATION

Car Parking: Please see below
Coach Parking: Please contact the club for information
Nearest Railway Station: Haydon's Road (½ mile)
Nearest Tube Station: Tooting Broadway/Wimbledon Park (both 1 mile)
Club Shop: At the Stadium
Opening Times: Monday-Friday 10.00am to 5.00pm
Telephone Nº: (020) 8547-3528

GROUND INFORMATION

Away Supporters' Entrances & Sections:
Please contact the club for information

ADMISSION INFO (2024/2025 PRICES)

Adult Seating: £23.00 – £32.00
Concessionary Seating: £16.00 – £28.00
Under-17s Seating: £5.00 – £18.00

FANS WITH DISABILITIES INFORMATION

Wheelchairs: Accommodated
Helpers: Admitted
Prices: Please contact the club for information
Disabled Toilets: Available
Contact: (020) 8547-3528   (Bookings are necessary)

Travelling Supporters' Information:
Routes: As there is no parking available near to the Stadium, and the area is very well served by public transport, Supporters are advised to travel to matches by bus, tube or rail, all of which operate services close to the ground.

BARROW AFC

Founded: 1901 (**Re-entered League**: 2020)
Former Names: None
Nickname: 'Bluebirds'
Ground: The SO Legal Stadium, Wilkie Road,
Barrow-in-Furness   LA14 5UW
Record Attendance: 16,874 (vs Swansea City, 1954)

Colours: White shirts with Blue sleeves, Blue shorts
Telephone Nº: (01229) 666010
Ground Capacity: 5,045
Seating Capacity: 1,000
Website: www.barrowafc.com
E-mail: office@barrowafc.com

GENERAL INFORMATION

Car Parking: Street Parking, Popular Side Car Park and
Soccer Bar Car Park
Coach Parking: Adjacent to the ground
Nearest Railway Station: Barrow Central (½ mile)
Nearest Bus Station: ½ mile (Bus No. 3 stops at the ground)
Club Shop: At the ground
Opening Times: Monday to Friday 9.00am to 4.00pm and
Saturday Home Matchdays 12.00pm to 2.55pm.
Telephone Nº: (01229) 666010

GROUND INFORMATION

Away Supporters' Entrances & Sections:
Holker Street End (uncovered terrace)

ADMISSION INFO (2024/2025 PRICES)

Adult Standing: £18.00
Adult Seating: £20.00
Concessionary Standing: £15.00
Concessionary Seating: £17.00
Ages 18 to 21 Standing/Seating: £17.00
Ages 7 to 17 Standing/Seating: £7.00
Concessionary Seating: Under-7s are admitted free with a
paying Adult.

DISABLED INFORMATION

Wheelchairs: 6 spaces available in the Disabled Area
Helpers: Admitted
Prices: Normal prices apply
Disabled Toilets: Available
Contact: (01229) 666010   (Bookings are not necessary)

Travelling Supporters' Information:
Routes: Exit the M6 at Junction 36 and take the A590 through Ulverston. Using the bypass, follow signs for Barrow. After
approximately 5 miles, turn left into Wilkie Road and the ground is on the right.

BRADFORD CITY FC

Founded: 1903 (**Entered League**: 1903)
Nickname: 'Bantams'
Ground: The University of Bradford Stadium, Valley Parade, Bradford BD8 7DY
Ground Capacity: 24,840 (All seats)
Record Attendance: 39,146 (11th March 1911)

Colours: Claret and Amber Striped shirts with Black shorts and socks
Telephone Nº: (01274) 773355
Ticket Office: (01274) 770012
Website: www.bradfordcityafc.com
E-mail: hello@bradfordcityafc.com

GENERAL INFORMATION

Car Parking: Street Parking and Car Parks (£3.00 charge)
Coach Parking: By Police direction
Nearest Railway Station: Bradford Foster Square
Nearest Bus Station: Bradford Interchange (1 mile)
Club Shop: At the ground
Opening Times: Monday to Friday 9.30am to 5.00pm and Saturday 10.00am to 3.00pm
Telephone Nº: (01274) 734521
Shop Website: www.bantams.clubstore.co.uk

GROUND INFORMATION

Away Supporters' Entrances & Sections:
Blocks F and G in the Mamma Mia (East) Stand (entrances on Midland Road)

ADMISSION INFO (2024/2025 PRICES)

Adult Seating: £25.00 (£20.00 purchased in advance)
Senior Citizen/Ages 17 to 23 Seating: £20.00
Under-17s Seating: £10.00
Note: Under-11s are admitted for £5.00 when accompanied by a paying adult – up to 3 Under-11s admitted per adult. (higher prices apply for upgrades to suites)

FANS WITH DISABILITIES INFORMATION

Wheelchairs: 100 spaces available in total for Home and Away fans throughout the ground. Access for away supporters is in the South Stand
Helpers: One helper admitted per fan with disabilities
Prices: Normal prices for fans with disabilities. Helpers free
Disabled Toilets: Available in all stands
Contact: 07818 515639 (Bookings are necessary)
Jamie Dorward (DLO) – jamiedorward@bradfordcityfc.co.uk

Travelling Supporters' Information: Routes: Exit the M62 at Junction 26 and take the M606 towards Bradford. At the end of the motorway get in the middle lane and follow signs for Bradford (West) into Rooley Lane (signs for the Airport). A McDonalds is now on your left. Turn left into Wakefield Road at the roundabout and stay in the middle lane. Continue straight on over two roundabouts (signs to Shipley and Skipton) onto Shipley Airedale Road which then becomes Canal Road. Just after Tesco on the left, turn left into Station Road and left again into Queens Road. Go up the hill to the third set of traffic lights and turn left into Manningham Lane. After the Gulf petrol station on the left, turn first left into Valley Parade for the Stadium.

BROMLEY FC

Founded: 1892 (**Entered League**: 2024)
Former Names: None
Nickname: 'The Ravens'
Ground: The Stadium, Hayes Lane, Bromley, Kent, BR2 9EF
Record Attendance: 10,798 (24th September 1949)

Colours: White shirts with Black shorts
Telephone N°: (020) 8460-5291
Ground Capacity: 5,000
Seating Capacity: 1,300
Website: www.bromleyfc.co.uk
E-mail: info@bromleyfc.co.uk

GENERAL INFORMATION

Car Parking: 300 spaces available at the ground
Coach Parking: At the ground
Nearest Railway Station: Bromley South (1 mile)
Nearest Bus Station: High Street, Bromley
Club Shop: At the ground
Opening Times: Matchdays only
Telephone N°: (020) 8460-5291

GROUND INFORMATION

Away Supporters' Entrances & Sections:
No usual segregation

ADMISSION INFO (2024/2025 PRICES)

Adult Standing/Seating: £20.00 (£24.00)
Concessionary Standing/Seating: £15.00 (£19.00)
Under-18s/Student Standing/Seating: £7.00 (£11.00)
Under-12s Standing/Seating: £5.00 (£7.00)
Note: Prices shown are for tickets purchased in advance.
Tickets purchased just before the game are more expensive
(prices shown above in brackets). Discounted prices are
available on the matchday for online bookings before
1.30pm or 6.30pm for day and night matches respectively.

DISABLED INFORMATION

Wheelchairs: Accommodated
Prices: Concessionary prices are charged for disabled fans.
Helpers are admitted free of charge
Disabled Toilets: Available
Contact: (0181) 460-5291 (Bookings are necessary)

Travelling Supporters' Information:
Routes: Exit the M25 at Junction 4 and follow the A21 for Bromley and London for approximately 4 miles before forking left onto the A232 signposted for Croydon/Sutton. At the second set of traffic lights turn right into Baston Road (B265) and follow for approximately 2 miles as it becomes Hayes Street and then Hayes Lane. The ground is on the right just after a mini-roundabout.

CARLISLE UNITED FC

Founded: 1903 (**Entered League**: 1928)
Former Names: Formed with the amalgamation of Shaddongate United FC and Carlisle Red Rose FC
Nickname: 'Cumbrians' 'Blues'
Ground: Brunton Park Stadium, Warwick Road, Carlisle CA1 1LL
Ground Capacity: 17,300
Seating Capacity: 7,594

Record Attendance: 27,500 (5th January 1957)
Colours: Royal Blue shirts and shorts
Telephone Nº: 0330 094-5930
Ticket Office: 0330 094-5930 Option 1
Website: www.carlisleunited.co.uk
E-mail: enquiries@carlisleunited.co.uk

GENERAL INFORMATION
Car Parking: Rear of Ground via St. Aidans Road (£3.00)
Coach Parking: St. Aidans Road Car Park
Nearest Railway Station: Carlisle Citadel (1 mile)
Nearest Bus Station: Lowther Street, Carlisle
Club Shop: At the ground
Opening Times: Monday to Friday 10.00am – 5.00pm (and until 7.45pm for evening matches). Saturday Matchdays open 10.00am to 5.30pm (but closes at 3.00pm on other Saturdays).
Telephone Nº: 0330 094-5930 Option 2

GROUND INFORMATION
Away Supporters' Entrances & Sections:
North End (Blocks 2 and 3) of the Pioneer Stand

ADMISSION INFO (2024/2025 PRICES)
Adult Standing: £23.00   **Seating**: £26.00
Senior Citizen Standing: £20.00   **Seating**: £23.00
Under-23s Standing: £17.00   **Seating**: £20.00
Under-18s Standing: £10.00   **Seating**: £13.00
Under-11s Standing/Seating: £7.00 – £10.00
Under-7s: £6.00 (free on Terrace with an adult)
Note: Tickets are cheaper if purchased before the matchday

FANS WITH DISABILITIES INFORMATION
Wheelchairs: 20 spaces for wheelchairs in a special section.
Helpers: One helper admitted per fan with disabilities
Prices: Fans in wheelchairs are admitted for £23.00. Helpers are admitted free of charge.
Disabled Toilets: Available throughout the ground
Contact: 07891 779015 Louise Banks (Bookings are recommended). E-mail: louise.banks@carlisleunited.co.uk

Travelling Supporters' Information:
Routes: From the North, South and East: Exit the M6 at Junction 43 and follow signs for Carlisle (A69) into Warwick Road for the ground; From the West: Take the A69 straight into Warwick Road.

CHELTENHAM TOWN FC

Founded: 1887
Nickname: 'Robins'
Ground: Completely-Suzukie Stadium,
Whaddon Road, Cheltenham   GL52 5NA
Ground Capacity: 7,200
Seating Capacity: 4,168

Record Attendance: 8,326 (1956)
Colours: Red and White striped shirts, White shorts
Telephone Nº: (01242) 573558
Ticket Office: (01242) 573558 Option 1
Website: www.ctfc.com
E-mail: info@ctfc.com

GENERAL INFORMATION

Car Parking: Available at the ground for a £6.00 charge
Coach Parking: Please phone for details
Nearest Railway Station: Cheltenham Spa (2½ miles)
Nearest Bus Station: Cheltenham Royal Well
Club Shop: At the ground
Opening Times: Tuesday, Thursday and Friday 10.00am to 3.00pm. Also Saturday Matchdays from 12.00pm.
Telephone Nº: (01242) 573558 Option 2

GROUND INFORMATION

Away Supporters' Entrances & Sections:
Hazlewoods Stand (entrance from Whaddon Road)

ADMISSION INFO (2024/2025 PRICES)

Adult Standing: £20.00
Adult Seating: £25.00 – £28.00
Concessionary Standing: £15.00
Concessionary Seating: £18.00 or £20.00
Under-18s Standing: £9.00
Under-18s Seating: £11.00 – £12.00

FANS WITH DISABILITIES INFORMATION

Wheelchairs: Accommodated in front of the Main Stand (use main entrance) and in the Colin Farmer Stand
Helpers: Admitted free of charge
Prices: Normal prices are charged
Disabled Toilets: Available in the Colin Farmer Stand, adjacent to the Main Stand and in the Social Club
Contact: (01242) 573558 (Bookings are necessary) – slo@ctfc.com

Travelling Supporters' Information:
Routes: The ground is situated to the North-East of Cheltenham, 1 mile from the Town Centre off the B4632 (Prestbury Road) – Whaddon Road is to the East of the B4632 just North of Pittville Circus. Road signs in the vicinity indicate 'Whaddon Road/ Cheltenham Town FC'.

CHESTERFIELD FC

Founded: 1866
Former Names: Chesterfield Municipal FC, Chesterfield Town FC
Nickname: 'Spireites' 'Blues'
Ground: SMH Group Stadium, 1866 Sheffield Road, Whittington Moor, Chesterfield   S41 8NZ
Ground Capacity: 10,600 (All seats)

Record Attendance: 10,108 (20th April 2024)
Colours: Blue shirts with White shorts
Telephone Nº: (01246) 269300
Ticket Office: (01246) 269300 (Option 1)
Website: www.chesterfield-fc.co.uk
E-mail: hello@chesterfield-fc.co.uk

GENERAL INFORMATION

Car Parking: Various Car Parks available nearby
Coach Parking: At the ground
Nearest Railway Station: Chesterfield (1¼ miles)
Nearest Bus Station: Chesterfield
Club Shop: At the ground
Opening Times: Please contact the club for details
Telephone Nº: (01246) 209765

GROUND INFORMATION

Away Supporters' Entrances & Sections:
H. Lilleker North Stand Turnstiles

ADMISSION INFO (2024/2025 PRICES)

Adult Seating: £20.00 – £24.00
Concessionary Seating: £18.00 – £22.00
Ages 17 to 21 Seating: £17.00 – £21.00
Ages 14 to 16 Seating: £11.00 – £12.00
Juvenile (Under-14s) Seating: £9.00 – £10.00
Under-7s Seating: £7.00 in the Family Stand

FANS WITH DISABILITIES INFORMATION

Wheelchairs: Up to 96 spaces available around the ground
Note: Lifts are available in the East and West stands
Helpers: One helper admitted per fan with disabilities
Prices: Normal prices for disabled fans. Free for helpers.
Disabled Toilets: Available in all stands
Contact: (01246) 269300 (Bookings are advised)

Travelling Supporters' Information:
Routes: From the South: Exit the M1 at Junction 29 and follow the A617 for Chesterfield. At the roundabout, take the 4th exit and head north on the A61 Sheffield Road and the stadium is located in the Whittington Moor district next to the junction with the A619; From the East: Take the A619 to Chesterfield and the ground is situated next to the Tesco supermarket at the junction with the A61; From the North: Exit the M1 at Junction 30 and take the A619 to Chesterfield. Then as above.

COLCHESTER UNITED FC

Founded: 1937 (**Entered League**: 1950)
Former Names: The Eagles FC & Colchester Town FC
Nickname: 'U's'
Ground: Jobserve Community Stadium,
United Way, Colchester   CO4 5UP
Ground Capacity: 10,105 (All seats)
Record Attendance: 19,072 (27/11/48 – Layer Road)

Colours: Royal blue and white striped shirts with
White shorts
Telephone Nº: (01206) 755100
Ticket Office: (01206) 755161
Website: www.colchesterunited.net
E-mail: media@colchesterunited.net

GENERAL INFORMATION

Car Parking: 700 spaces at the ground – pre-bookings only.
The club recommends the use of the Park and Ride car park
(access via Junction 28 of the A12 – Postcode CO4 5JA).
The stadium is a 5-10 minute walk over Boxted Road bridge
and the parking fee is £3.00.
Coach Parking: Drivers should liaise with with stewards
upon arrival at the ground
Nearest Railway Station: Colchester North (1½ miles)
Nearest Bus Station: Colchester Town Centre (1½ miles)
Club Shop: At the ground
Opening Times: Weekdays 10.00am to 2.00pm, Saturday
Matchdays 11.00am to 6.00pm and Midweek Matchdays
5.30pm to 10.00pm.
Telephone Nº: (01206) 755135

GROUND INFORMATION

Away Supporters' Entrances & Sections:
North Stand or East Stand (North End)

ADMISSION INFO (2024/2025 PRICES)

Adult Seating: £24.75 – £33.75
Concessionary Seating: £19.15 – £27.00
Ages 18 to 21 Seating: £19.15 – £27.00
Under-18s Seating: £15.25 – £18.50
Under-14s Seating: £6.00 – £9.50
Under-11s Seating: Free of charge
Note: A variety of discounted rates are available for tickets
purchased a set number of weeks in advance of the game.

FANS WITH DISABILITIES INFORMATION

Wheelchairs: 40 spaces in total situated in all stands with
lift access available where required.
Helpers: One helper admitted per wheelchair
Prices: Concessionary prices for fans with disabilities.
Helpers are admitted free of charge.
Disabled Toilets: Available in each stand
Contact: (01206) 755161 or (01206) 755130 (Disability
Liaison Officer: chris.saward@colchesterunited.net)

Travelling Supporters' Information:
Routes: The stadium is located just to the south of junction 28 of the A12 on the northern outskirts of Colchester. As parking
near the stadium is limited, the club recommends the use of the Park and Ride car park which is situated just to the north of
junction 28. The stadium is then a 5 to 10 minute walk. Alternatively, pre-book a space in the club car park.

CREWE ALEXANDRA FC

Founded: 1877 (**Entered League**: 1892)
Nickname: 'Railwaymen'
Ground: Alexandra Stadium, Gresty Road, Crewe, Cheshire   CW2 6EB
Ground Capacity: 10,101 (All seats)
Record Attendance: 20,000 (30th January 1960)

Colours: Red shirts with White shorts
Telephone N°: (01270) 213014
Ticket Office: (01270) 252610
Website: www.crewealex.net
E-mail: info@crewealex.net

GENERAL INFORMATION

Car Parking: Car Park at the ground (spaces for 400 cars with a £3.50 fee)
Coach Parking: Car Park at the ground
Nearest Railway Station: Crewe (5 minutes walk)
Nearest Bus Station: Crewe Town
Club Shop: At the ground
Opening Times: Monday to Friday and Matchdays 9.00am – 5.00pm (until 7.45pm for Night matches)
Telephone N°: (01270) 213014 Option 2

GROUND INFORMATION

Away Supporters' Entrances & Sections:
Whitby Morrison Ice Cream Van Stand

ADMISSION INFO (2024/2025 PRICES)

Adult Seating: £26.00 – £28.00
Concessionary Seating: £20.00 – £22.00
Under-17s Seating: £11.50 – £13.50
Under-11s Seating: £1.00
Note: Members' prices are cheaper

FANS WITH DISABILITIES INFORMATION

Wheelchairs: Over 70 spaces are available for home fans and 14 spaces are available for away fans
Helpers: One helper admitted per fan with disabilities
Prices: £22.00 for each fan with disabilities and one helper
Disabled Toilets: Available in all Stands
Commentaries are available for the blind
Contact: (01270) 252610 or 07733 077611
Beverley Dyer – bdyer@crewealex.net   (Bookings necessary)

Travelling Supporters' Information:
Routes: From the North: Exit the M6 at Junction 17 and take the Crewe (A534) road, and at Crewe roundabout follow signs for Chester into Nantwich Road. Then take a left turn into Gresty Road; From the South and East: Take the A52 to the A5020, then on to Crewe roundabout (then as from the North); From the West: Take the A534 into Crewe and turn right just before the railway station into Gresty Road.   **SatNav users**: Please enter the following post code: CW2 6EB

DONCASTER ROVERS FC

Founded: 1879
Former Names: None
Nickname: 'Rovers'
Ground: Eco-Power Stadium, Stadium Way, Doncaster DN4 5JW
Record Attendance: 15,001 (1st April 2008)

Colours: Red & White hooped shirts with White shorts
Telephone N°: (01302) 764664
Ticket Office: (01302) 762576
Ground Capacity: 15,231 (All seats)
Website: www.doncasterroversfc.co.uk
E-mail: info@clubdoncaster.co.uk

GENERAL INFORMATION

Car Parking: 1,000 spaces available at the ground (£5.00)
Coach Parking: At the ground (£20.00 fee)
Nearest Railway Station: Doncaster (2 miles)
Nearest Bus Station: Doncaster (2 miles)
Club Shop: At the ground
Opening Times: Monday to Saturday 10.00am to 4.00pm (until 8.00pm for midweek matches). Saturday Matchdays open 10.00am to kick-off then from full-time until 5.30pm.
Telephone N°: (01302) 764667

GROUND INFORMATION

Away Supporters' Entrances & Sections:
Ellgia (North) Stand

ADMISSION INFO (2024/2025 PRICES)

Adult Seating: £21.00 – £22.00
Senior Citizen/Ages 22 to 24 Seating: £17.00 – £18.00
Ages 18 to 24 Seating: £17.00 – £18.00
Ages 14 to 17 Seating: £10.00
Under-14s Seating: £5.00
Note: Members prices and advance purchases are lower than those shown.

FANS WITH DISABILITIES INFORMATION

Wheelchairs: 18 spaces available in total with Away fans accommodated in the North Stand
Helpers: Admitted
Prices: Normal prices for fans with disabilities. Helpers are admitted free of charge
Disabled Toilets: Available in all Stands (Radar Key required)
Contact: (01302) 764668 (Bookings necessary)
Dan Breslin (DLO) dan.breslin@clubdoncaster.co.uk

Travelling Supporters' Information:
Routes: Exit the M18 at Junction 3 and follow the A6182 towards Doncaster. The stadium is approximately 1½ miles from the motorway and is well signposted so follow these signs. There are 1,000 car parking spaces available at the stadium and the cost is £5.00 per car. A number of businesses on the nearby business park also offer matchday parking for a similar charge.
Bus services run from the town centre/interchange to the Stadium with a shuttle service back operating after the match.

FLEETWOOD TOWN FC

Founded: 1997   (**Entered League**: 2012)
Former Names: Fleetwood FC (1908-1976), Fleetwood Town FC (1977-1996), Fleetwood Freeport FC (1997-2002)
Nickname: 'Cod Army'
Ground: Highbury Stadium, Park Avenue, Fleetwood   FY7 6TX
Record Attendance: 6,150 vs Rochdale (13/11/65)

Colours: Red shirts with White arms, White shorts
Telephone N°: (01253) 775080
Ground Capacity: 5,137
Seating Capacity: 2,701
Website: www.fleetwoodtownfc.com
E-mail: info@fleetwoodtownfc.com

GENERAL INFORMATION

Car Parking: Street parking only
Coach Parking: Drop off in Hatfield Road (FY7 7DT) then park opposite the Steamer Pub on Queen's Terrace (FY7 6BT)
Nearest Railway Station: Poulton-le-Fylde (7 miles)
Nearest Bus Station: No.1 and No.14 buses from Blackpool town centre (30 minute journey)
Nearest Tram Stop from Blackpool: Stanley Road
Club Shop: At the ground and Poolfoot Farm Sports Complex
Opening Times: Monday to Friday 9.00am to 5.00pm
Telephone N°: (01253) 775080

GROUND INFORMATION

Away Supporters' Entrances & Sections:
Percy Ronson Terrace (turnstiles 1-3) for standing and Parkside Stand seating (turnstiles 1-2)

ADMISSION INFO (2024/2025 PRICES)

Adult Standing: £24.00
Adult Seating: £26.00
Senior Citizen/Under-25s Standing: £19.00
Senior Citizen/Under-25s Seating: £21.00
Under-16s Standing: £9.00
Under-16s Seating: £10.00 – £11.00
Note: Prices are cheaper for members

FANS WITH DISABILITIES INFORMATION

Wheelchairs: Accommodated
Helpers: Admitted
Prices: Normal prices for the fans with disabilities. Free of charge for helpers
Disabled Toilets: Available
Contact: (01253) 775080   (Bookings are necessary)

Travelling Supporters' Information:
Routes: Exit the M6 at Junction 32 and take the M55 towards Blackpool. Exit the M55 at Junction 3 and follow the A585 towards Fleetwood for approximately 11½ miles. On the outskirts of town, you will reach a roundabout with Blackpool and Fylde college on your left. Continue straight on at this roundabout but then take the first turn on the left into Copse Road. After approximately 1 mile, branch left and turn left onto Radcliffe Road as you pass the Fire Station. Take the next right onto Stanley Road and the Stadium is at the bottom of the road on the left.

GILLINGHAM FC

Founded: 1893 (**Entered League**: 1920)
Former Names: New Brompton FC (1893-1913)
Nickname: 'Gills'
Ground: MEMS Priestfield Stadium, Redfern Avenue, Gillingham, Kent ME7 2PE
Ground Capacity: 11,582 (All seats)

Record Attendance: 23,002 (10th January 1948)
Telephone Nº: (01634) 300000
Ticket Office: (01634) 300000
Website: www.gillinghamfootballclub.com
E-mail: info@gillinghamfootballclub.com

GENERAL INFORMATION

Car Parking: Street parking
Coach Parking: Croneen's Yard Car Park in Railway Street (5 minute walk)
Nearest Railway Station: Gillingham
Nearest Bus Station: Gillingham
Club Shop: Megastore in Redfern Avenue
Opening Times: Megastore is open Weekdays from 9.00am to 5.00pm and Matchdays from 9.00am to 3.00pm
Telephone Nº: (01634) 300000

GROUND INFORMATION

Away Supporters' Entrances & Sections:
Priestfield Road End

ADMISSION INFO (2024/2025 PRICES)

Adult Seating: £23.00 – £26.00
Senior Citizen Seating: £20.00 – £23.00
Ages 18 to 21 Seating: £15.00 – £18.00
Under-18s Seating: £11.00 – £14.00
Under-14s Seating: £8.00 – £11.00

FANS WITH DISABILITIES INFORMATION

Wheelchairs: 67 spaces in total for Home and Away fans and helpers in special sections around the ground
Helpers: One helper admitted per fan with disabilities
Prices: Normal prices for fans with disabilities. Helpers free
Disabled Toilets: Available in all areas of the ground
Contact: (01634) 300000 (Bookings are necessary)
Disability Liaison Officer: Ben Reeves – breeves@priestfield.com

Travelling Supporters' Information:
Routes: From All Parts: Exit the M2 at Junction 4 and follow the link road (dual carriageway) B278 to the 3rd roundabout. Turn left onto the A2 (dual carriageway) and go across the roundabout to the traffic lights. Turn right into Woodlands Road after the traffic lights. The ground is ¼ mile on the left.

GRIMSBY TOWN FC

Founded: 1878   (**Entered League**: 1890)
Former Names: Grimsby Pelham FC (1879)
Nickname: 'Mariners'
Ground: Blundell Park, Cleethorpes   DN35 7PY
Ground Capacity: 8,933 (All seats)
Record Attendance: 31,651 (20th February 1937)

Colours: Black and White striped shirts, Black shorts
Telephone Nº: (01472) 605050
Ticket Office: (01472) 605050 (Option 4)
Website: www.gtfc.co.uk
E-mail: enquiries@gtfc.co.uk

GENERAL INFORMATION

Car Parking: Street parking
Coach Parking: Harrington Street – near the ground
Nearest Railway Station: Cleethorpes (1½ miles)
Nearest Bus Station: Brighowgate, Grimsby (4 miles)
Club Shop: At the ground
Opening Times: Monday – Saturday 10.00am to 2.00pm
but closed on Saturday Matchdays at present
Telephone Nº: (01472) 605050   Option 1

GROUND INFORMATION

Away Supporters' Entrances & Sections:
Harrington Street turnstiles 15-18 and Constitution Avenue
turnstiles 5-14 for accommodation in the Osmond Stand

ADMISSION INFO (2024/2025 PRICES)

Adult Seating: £26.00
Senior Citizen/Student Seating: £17.00
Ages 14 to 17 Seating: £8.00
Under-14s Seating: £6.00 – £8.00
Note: Some tickets are cheaper if purchased before the
matchday

FANS WITH DISABILITIES INFORMATION

Wheelchairs: 20 spaces for home fans in the Main Stand
and 20 spaces for away fans in the Osmond Stand
Helpers: Helpers are admitted
Prices: Normal prices for fans with disabilities. Helpers free
Disabled Toilets: Available in Main Stand
Commentaries are also available
Contact: (01472) 605050   (Bookings are necessary)
Amanda Jane Stephenson – janestephenson@gtfc.co.uk

Travelling Supporters' Information:
Routes: From All Parts except Lincolnshire and East Anglia: Take the M180 to the A180 and follow signs for Grimsby/
Cleethorpes. The A180 ends at a roundabout (the 3rd in short distance after crossing docks), take the 2nd exit from the roundabout
over the Railway flyover into Cleethorpes Road (A1098) and continue into Grimsby Road. After the second stretch of dual
carriageway, the ground is ½ mile on the left; From Lincolnshire: Take the A46 or A16 and follow Cleethorpes signs along
(A1098) Weelsby Road for 2 miles. Take the 1st exit at the roundabout at the end of Clee Road into Grimsby Road. The ground is
1¾ miles on the right.

HARROGATE TOWN AFC

Founded: 1919 (**Entered League**: 2020)
Former Names: Harrogate FC and Harrogate Hotspurs FC
Nickname: 'Town'
Ground: Environvent Stadium, Wetherby Road, Harrogate HG2 7SA
Record Attendance: 15,000 (vs Sheffield Utd, 1920)

Colours: Yellow and Black striped shirts, Black shorts
Telephone Nº: (01423) 210600
Ground Capacity: 5,000
Seating Capacity: 1,500
Website: www.harrogatetownafc.com
E-mail: enquiries@harrogatetownafc.com

GENERAL INFORMATION

Car Parking: At the Kingsway Surgery on Wetherby Road or Cedar Court Hotel on Park Parade (£5.00 charge)
Coach Parking: At the ground
Nearest Railway Station: Harrogate (¾ mile)
Nearest Bus Station: Harrogate
Club Shop: At the ground
Opening Times: Monday to Friday 9.00am to 3.00pm and also on Matchdays
Telephone Nº: (01423) 210600

GROUND INFORMATION

Away Supporters' Entrances & Sections:
No usual segregation

ADMISSION INFO (2024/2025 PRICES)

Adult Standing: £24.00   **Adult Seating**: £27.00
Concessionary Standing: £18.00
Concessionary Seating: £21.00
Under-18s Standing: £10.00   **Seating**: £13.00
Under-12s Standing: £8.00   **Seating**: £11.00
Under-5s Standing/Seating: £4.00
Note: Tickets are cheaper when purchased in advance.

DISABLED INFORMATION

Wheelchairs: Accommodated at the front of the Main Stand
Helpers: One helper admitted for each disabled fan
Prices: Free of charge for each disabled fan and helper
Disabled Toilets: Available
Contact: (01423) 210600   (Bookings are necessary)

Travelling Supporters' Information:
Routes: From the South: Take the A61 from Leeds and turn right at the roundabout onto the ring road (signposted York). After about 1¼ miles turn left at the next roundabout onto A661 Wetherby Road. The ground is situated ¾ mile on the right; From the West: Take the A59 straight into Wetherby Road from Empress Roundabout and the ground is on the left; From the East & North: Exit the A1(M) at Junction 47, take the A59 to Harrogate then follow the Southern bypass to Wetherby Road for the A661 Roundabout. Turn right towards Harrogate Town Centre and the ground is on the right after ¾ mile.

MILTON KEYNES DONS FC

Founded: 2004
Former Names: None
Nickname: 'Dons'
Ground: Stadium MK, Stadium Way West,
Milton Keynes   MK1 1ST
Ground Capacity: 30,500 (All seats)

Record Attendance: 28,521
(vs Liverpool, 25th September 2019)
Colours: White shirts and shorts
Telephone Nº: (01908) 622922
Ticket Office: (01908) 622933
Website: www.mkdons.com
E-mail: info@mkdons.com

GENERAL INFORMATION

Car Parking: 1,600 Pay and Display spaces at Stadium MK
(£7.00 charge). Disabled drivers can park free of charge on
production of a valid blue badge (entry via Saxon Street).
Coach Parking: By Police direction
Nearest Railway Station: Bletchley (1 mile)
Nearest Bus Station: Bletchley
Club Shop: At the Stadium
Opening Times: Weekdays 10.00am to 4.00pm
Telephone Nº: (01908) 622973

GROUND INFORMATION

Away Supporters' Entrances & Sections:
North Stand corner, Gate 3

ADMISSION INFO (2024/2025 PRICES)

Adult Seating: £24.00 – £36.00
Concessionary Seating: £18.00 – £27.00
Ages 22 to 24 Seating: £12.00 – £27.00
Ages 14 to 21 Seating: £6.00 – £18.00
Under-14s Seating: £3.00 – £9.00

FANS WITH DISABILITIES INFORMATION

Wheelchairs: A total of 123 spaces are available around the
ground at concourse level, 93 for home fans, 20 for away fans
Helpers: One helper admitted per fan with disabilities
Prices: Normal prices for fans with disabilities. Helpers are
admitted free of charge
Disabled Toilets: Available throughout the stadium
Contact: (01908) 622999   (Bookings are necessary) –
E-mail: disability@mkdons.com or contact Andy Standen
andy.standen@stadiummk.com

Travelling Supporters' Information:
Routes: From all parts: Exit the M1 at Junction 14, following signs for Milton Keynes and cross the first roundabout onto H6
Childs Way. Turn left at the next roundabout onto V11 Tongwell Street. Continue along this road then turn right at the third
roundabout onto H9 Groveway. Continue along Groveway then take the first exit at the fourth roundabout towards Central
Bletchley. Stadium:MK is the first turning on the left.

MORECAMBE FC

Founded: 1920 (**Entered League**: 2007)
Former Names: None
Nickname: 'Shrimps'
Ground: The Mazuma Mobile Stadium, Christie Way,
Westgate, Morecambe   LA4 4TB
Record Attendance: 9,324 (1962 – Christie Park)

Colours: Red shirts with Red shorts
Telephone N°: (01524) 411797
Ground Capacity: 6,476
Seating Capacity: 2,173
Website: www.morecambefc.com
E-mail: office@morecambefc.com

GENERAL INFORMATION

Car Parking: Available at a school adjacent to the ground
Coach Parking: Available at the rear of the stadium
Nearest Railway Station: Morecambe Central (2 miles)
Nearest Bus Station: Morecambe
Club Shop: At the ground
Opening Times: Weekdays & Matchdays 9.00am to 5.00pm
Telephone N°: (01524) 411797 Option 3

GROUND INFORMATION

Away Supporters' Entrances & Sections:
Dennison Trailers (East) Away Stand plus seating in part of
the Main Stand.

ADMISSION INFO (2024/2025 PRICES)

Adult Standing: £20.00
Adult Seating: £25.00
Senior Citizen Standing: £15.00
Senior Citizen Seating: £20.00
Ages 18 to 22 Standing: £10.00
Ages 18 to 22 Seating: £15.00
Ages 14 to 17 Standing: £5.00
Ages 14 to 17 Seating: £7.00
Note: Under-14s must be accompanied by a paying adult
and pay £3.00 Standing or £5.00 Seating

FANS WITH DISABILITIES INFORMATION

Wheelchairs: Accommodated – 39 spaces available in total
Helpers: Admitted
Prices: Concessionary prices are charged for fans with
disabilities. Helpers are admitted free of charge
Disabled Toilets: Available in all stands
Contact: (01524) 411797   (Bookings are preferred)

Travelling Supporters' Information:
Routes: Exit the M6 at Junction 34 and follow signs to Morecambe. Cross the River Lune via the Greyhound Bridge and continue,
following signs for Morecambe onto the A589. At the first two roundabouts, keep in the right hand lane and carry straight on.
Turn left at the third roundabout (Shrimp) and continue along Westgate for about a mile. Globe Stadium is on the right.
Away fans car parking: Turn right after the Junior School towards Venture Caravan Park and the away car park is signposted.

NEWPORT COUNTY AFC

Founded: 1989   (**Entered League**: 2013)
Former Names: Newport AFC
Nickname: 'The Exiles'
Ground: Rodney Parade, Newport   NP19 0UU
Record Attendance: 9,836 (vs Tottenham Hotspur in January 2018 when temporary seating was erected)

Colours: Amber shirts with Black shorts
Telephone Nº: (01633) 302012
Ground Capacity: 7,850
Seating Capacity: 1,236
Website: www.newport-county.co.uk
E-mail: office@newport-county.co.uk

GENERAL INFORMATION

Car Parking: Street parking only
Coach Parking: By Police direction
Nearest Railway Station: Newport (½ mile)
Nearest Bus Station: Newport
Club Shop: At Kingsway Shopping Centre, Newport
Opening Times: Monday to Saturday 9.30am to 5.00pm (until 4.00pm on regular Saturdays). Saturday Matchdays 10.00am to 2.00pm.
Telephone Nº: (01633) 264572

GROUND INFORMATION

Away Supporters' Entrances & Sections:
Sytner End turnstiles for Bisley Stand accommodation

ADMISSION INFO (2024/2025 PRICES)

Adult Standing: £20.00
Adult Seating: £25.00
Senior Citizen Standing/Seating: £18.00
Ages 16 to 21 Standing: £14.00
Ages 16 to 21 Seating: £16.00
Under-16s Standing/Seating: £10.00
Under-12s Standing/Seating: £8.00

FANS WITH DISABILITIES INFORMATION

Wheelchairs: Accommodated – 11 spaces available in total
Helpers: Admitted
Prices: Normal prices for fans with disabilities. Helpers free
Disabled Toilets: 4 available
Contact: (01633) 415376   Rob Parsons (DLO)
E-mail: dob291176@hotmail.com

Travelling Supporters' Information:
Routes: From the West: Exit the M4 at Junction 26 of the M4 and take the 3rd exit at the roundabout onto Malpas Road. Take the 2nd exit at the next roundabout then the 1st exit at the following roundabout across the River Usk bridge. * At the next set of traffic lights bear right onto Chepstow Road, take the first right onto Cedar Road then the first right onto Corporation Road. Take the next left onto Grafton Road and Rodney Parade is on left hand side; From The East: Exit the M4 at Junction 25A and take the 1st exit at the roundabout onto Heidenheim Way. Take the 1st exit off the fly-over then the 2nd exit at the first roundabout then the 1st exit at the next roundabout across the River Usk bridge. Then as above *.

NOTTS COUNTY FC

Founded: 1862 (**Entered League**: 1888)
Nickname: 'The Magpies'
Ground: Meadow Lane Stadium, Nottingham, NG2 3HJ
Ground Capacity: 19,841 (All seats)
Record Attendance: 47,310 (12th March 1955)

Colours: Black and White striped shirts, Black shorts
Telephone Nº: (0115) 952-9000
Ticket Office: (0115) 955-7210
Website: www.nottscountyfc.co.uk
E-mail: office@nottscountyfc.co.uk

GENERAL INFORMATION

Car Parking: Meadow Lane and Cattle Market
Coach Parking: Incinerator Road (Cattle Market Corner)
Nearest Railway Station: Nottingham (½ mile)
Nearest Bus Station: Broadmarsh Centre (Station Street)
Club Shop: At the ground
Opening Times: Mondays to Friday 9.00am – 5.00pm, Saturday Matchdays 9.00am until half-time, other Saturdays 9.00am – 1.00pm
Telephone Nº: (0115) 955-7200

GROUND INFORMATION

Away Supporters' Entrances & Sections:
Jimmy Sirrel Stand, Block Z – use Turnstiles 19-24

ADMISSION INFO (2024/2025 PRICES)

Adult Seating: £27.50
Senior Citizen Seating: £21.50
Ages 18 to 21 Seating: £21.50
Under-18s Seating: £13.50
Under-16s Seating: £11.50
Under-12s Seating: £7.50
Note: Discounted prices are available for advance purchases

DISABLED INFORMATION

Wheelchairs: 34 spaces for home fans in the Derek Pavis Stand and Haydn Green Family Stand and 10 spaces for away fans in the Jimmy Sirrel Stand
Helpers: One helper admitted with each disabled fan
Prices: Normal prices apply for fans with disabilities.
Disabled Toilets: Available throughout the ground
Contact: (0115) 955-7241 (Bookings are necessary)
slo@nottscountyfc.co.uk

Travelling Supporters' Information:
Routes: From the North: Exit the M1 at Junction 26 following Nottingham signs (A610) then Melton Mowbray and Trent Bridge (A606) signs. Before the River Trent turn left into Meadow Lane; From the South: Exit the M1 at Junction 24 following signs for Nottingham (South) to Trent Bridge, cross the river and follow the one-way system to the right, then turn left and right at the traffic lights then second right into Meadow Lane; From the East: Take the A52 to West Bridgford/Trent Bridge, cross the river and follow the one-way system to the right then turn left and right at the traffic lights, then second right into Meadow Lane; From the West: Take the A52 into Nottingham following signs for Melton Mowbray and Trent Bridge. Before the River Trent turn left into Meadow Lane.

PORT VALE FC

Founded: 1876 (**Entered League**: 1892)
Former Names: Burslem Port Vale FC
Nickname: 'Valiants'
Ground: Vale Park, Hamil Road, Burslem,
Stoke-on-Trent ST6 1AW
Ground Capacity: 19,052 (All seats)
Record Attendance: 49,768 (20nd February 1960)

Colours: White shirts with Black detail, Black shorts
Telephone N°: (01782) 655800
Ticket Office: (01782) 655821
Website: www.port-vale.co.uk
E-mail: enquiries@port-vale.co.uk

GENERAL INFORMATION

Car Parking: Car parks at the ground (£5.00)
Coach Parking: Hamil Road car park (£25.00)
Nearest Railway Station: Stoke
Nearest Bus Station: Burslem (adjacent)
Club Shop: At the ground
Opening Times: Monday to Friday 9.00am – 5.00pm and
Saturday Matchdays 9.30am to 3.15pm
Telephone N°: (01782) 655822

GROUND INFORMATION

Away Supporters' Entrances & Sections:
Hamil Road turnstiles, numbers 1 to 8

ADMISSION INFO (2024/2025 PRICES)

Adult Seating: £25.00
Concessionary Seating: £20.00
Ages 18 to 21 Seating: £17.00
Ages 13 to 17 Seating: £12.00
Under-13s Seating: £2.00
Note: Discounted Family Tickets are available

FANS WITH DISABILITIES INFORMATION

Wheelchairs: 46 spaces available in a special area in the
Lorne Street/Bycars Corner
Helpers: One helper admitted per fan with disabilities
Prices: Normal prices for fans with disabilities. Helpers free
Disabled Toilets: Available
Commentaries are available – please contact the club
Contact: (01782) 655821 (Bookings are necessary) –
Luke Cassidy E-mail: dao@port-vale.co.uk

Travelling Supporters' Information:
Routes: From the North: Exit the M6 at Junction 16 and follow Stoke signs (A500). Branch left off the A500 at the exit signposted Tunstall and take the 2nd exit at the roundabout into Newcastle Street. Proceed through the traffic lights into Moorland Road and take the 2nd turning on the left into Hamil Road; From the South and West: Exit the M6 at Junction 15 and take the A5006 and A500. After 6¼ miles branch left (then as from the North); From the East: Take the A50 or A52 into Stoke following Burslem signs into Waterloo Road, turn right at Burslem crossroads into Moorland Road (then as from the North).

SALFORD CITY FC

Founded: 1940 (**Entered League**: 2019)
Former Names: Salford Central FC, Salford FC, Salford Amateurs FC plus some other early names
Nickname: 'The Ammies'
Ground: The Peninsula Stadium, Moor Lane, Salford, Manchester   M7 3PZ
Record Attendance: 4,518 (vs Leeds United, 13/8/19)

Colours: Red shirts with White shorts
Ground Capacity: 5,106
Seating Capacity: 2,246
Website: www.salfordcityfc.co.uk
E-mail: enquiries@salfordcityfc.co.uk

GENERAL INFORMATION

Car Parking: Limited street parking only. A resident permit zone is in place around the ground
Coach Parking: On Moor Lane outside the ground
Nearest Railway Station: Salford Crescent (2½ miles)
Nearest Bus Station: Services 97, 98 and X43 Witchway from Manchester City Centre stop near the ground
Club Shop: At the ground
Opening Times: Monday to Friday 10.00am to 4.00pm. Saturday matchdays 12.00pm until 30 minutes prior to kick-off. Tuesday matchdays 2.00pm until kick-off
Telephone Nº: ()161) 711-1164

GROUND INFORMATION

Away Supporters' Entrances & Sections:
East Stand Turnstiles Block A

ADMISSION INFO (2024/2025 PRICES)

Adult Standing/Seating: £15.00 – £22.00
Senior Citizen Standing/Seating: £12.00 – £19.00
Ages 18 to 21 Standing/Seating: £10.00 – £19.00
Ages 14 to 17 Standing/Seating: £10.00 – £16.00
Under-14s Standing/Seating: £5.00 – £10.00
Note: Prices vary depending on the category of the game.

FANS WITH DISABILITIES INFORMATION

Wheelchairs: Accommodated in the North & South Stands
Helpers: Admitted
Prices: Normal prices are charged for fans with disabilities. Helpers are admitted free of charge
Disabled Toilets: Available in the North & South Stands
Contact: (0161) 711-1164   (Bookings are not necessary) – tickets@salfordcityfc.co.uk

Travelling Supporters' Information:
Routes: Exit the M60 at Junction 17 and take the A56 Bury New Road towards Prestwich. Continue along, passing the A6044 (Hilton Lane) road then turn right along Moor Lane heading towards Kersal Moor and the Golf Course. The ground is on the left hand side of the road after a few hundred yards.

SWINDON TOWN FC

Founded: 1881 (**Entered League**: 1920)
Nickname: 'Robins'
Ground: The County Ground, County Road, Swindon   SN1 2ED
Ground Capacity: 15,547 (All seats)
Record Attendance: 32,000 (15th January 1972)

Colours: Red shirts and shorts
Telephone Nº: 0330 002-1879
Ticket Office: 0330 002-1879
Website: www.swindontownfc.co.uk
E-mail: reception@swindontownfc.co.uk

GENERAL INFORMATION

Car Parking: Town Centre, street Parking and local matchday car parks
Coach Parking: Car park adjacent to the ground
Nearest Railway Station: Swindon (½ mile)
Nearest Bus Station: Swindon (½ mile)
Club Shop: The Swindon Town Superstore
Opening Times: Weekdays 9.00am – 5.00pm, Non-Matchday Saturdays 9.00am – 12.00pm and Saturday Matchdays 9.00am to 6.00pm
Telephone Nº: 0330 002-1879

GROUND INFORMATION

Away Supporters' Entrances & Sections:
Arkell's Stand turnstiles for the Stratton Bank

ADMISSION INFO (2024/2025 PRICES)

Adult Seating: £21.00 – £24.00
Concessionary Seating: £18.00 – £20.00
Under-21s Seating: £12.00 – £14.00
Under-18s Seating: £8.00 – £10.00
Under-11s Seating: £3.00

FANS WITH DISABILITIES INFORMATION

Wheelchairs: 51 spaces in total for Home and Away fans in a special section in front of Arkell's Stand (45 home, 6 away)
Helpers: One helper admitted with each fan in a wheelchair
Prices: Concessionary prices for fans with disabilities. Helpers are admitted free of charge.
Disabled Toilets: Available
Commentaries are available for the blind
Contact: 0330 002-1879 (Bookings are necessary) – reception@swindontownafc.co.uk Caroline Lane (DLO)

Travelling Supporters' Information:
Routes: From London, the East and the South: Exit the M4 at Junction 15 and take the A345 into Swindon along Queen's Drive. Take the 3rd exit at 'Magic Roundabout' into County Road; From the West: Exit the M4 at Junction 15 then as above; From the North: Take the M4 or A345/A420/A361 to the County Road roundabout, then as above.

TRANMERE ROVERS FC

Founded: 1884
Former Name: Belmont FC
Nickname: 'Rovers' 'Super White Army'
Ground: Prenton Park, Prenton Road West, Birkenhead   CH42 9PY
Ground Capacity: 16,567 (All seats)

Record Attendance: 24,424 (5th February 1972)
Colours: White shirts with Blue shorts
Telephone Nº: 03330 144452
Ticket Office: 03330 144452 Option 2
Website: www.tranmererovers.co.uk
E-mail: via club's website

GENERAL INFORMATION

Car Parking: Large car park at the ground (£5.00 per car)
Coach Parking: At the ground (£10.00 charge)
Nearest Railway Stations: Hamilton Square, Rock Ferry and Conway Park (approximately 1½ miles)
Nearest Bus Station: Conway Park (Town Centre)
Club Shop: At the ground
Opening Times: Thursday to Saturday 9.00am to 5.00pm
Telephone Nº: 03330 144452 Option 1

GROUND INFORMATION

Away Supporters' Entrances & Sections:
Cowshed Stand turnstiles 5-9 – access from Borough Road (Away section capacity: 2,500)

ADMISSION INFO (2024/2025 PRICES)

Adult Seating: £25.00 – £28.00
Concessionary Seating: £20.00 – £23.00
Young Persons Seating (Ages 18-22): £18.00 – £21.00
Under-18s Seating: £11.00
Under-12s Seating: £7.00
Note: Discounted prices are available for advance purchases and executive areas have higher prices.

FANS WITH DISABILITIES INFORMATION

Wheelchairs: 54 spaces in total for Home and Away fans in the disabled section, Bebington Paddock
Helpers: One helper admitted per fan with disabilities
Prices: £18.00 – £21.00 for fans with disabilities (with a free ticket for a carer)
Disabled Toilets: 2 available in the disabled section
Contact: (0151) 609-3380 (Bookings are necessary) – christiner@tranmererovers.co.uk (Disability Liaison Officer)

Travelling Supporters' Information:
Routes: From the North: From Liverpool city centre, travel through the Kingsway (Wallasey) Mersey Tunnel (£1.70 toll for cars) then continue onto the M53, exiting at Junction 3. Take the first exit (signposted Birkenhead), continue past Sainsbury's then turn right at the traffic lights by the Halfway House pub then turn left into Prenton Road West at the next set of lights. The ground is on the right after a short distance. From the South: Exit the M53 at Junction 4 and take the 4th exit at the roundabout onto the B5151 Mount Road (the ground is signposted from here). After 2½ miles, turn right at the traffic lights (by the United Reformed Church) into Prenton Road West for the ground.

WALSALL FC

Founded: 1888 (**Entered League**: 1892)
Former Name: Walsall Town Swifts FC (1888-1895)
Nickname: 'Saddlers'
Ground: The Poundland Bescot Stadium, Bescot Crescent, Walsall, West Midlands WS1 4SA
Ground Capacity: 11,300 (All seats)

Record Attendance: 11,049 (9th May 2004)
Colours: Red shirts with White shorts
Telephone Nº: (01922) 622791
Ticket Office: (01922) 651416 or (01922) 651414
Website: www.saddlers.co.uk
E-mail: info@walsallfc.co.uk

GENERAL INFORMATION

Car Parking: Car park at the ground
Coach Parking: At the ground
Nearest Railway Station: Bescot (adjacent)
Nearest Bus Station: Bradford Place, Walsall
Club Shop: At the ground
Opening Times: Weekdays 9.00am – 4.30pm and Saturday Matchdays 10.00am to 5.30pm
Telephone Nº: (01922) 651410

GROUND INFORMATION

Away Supporters' Entrances & Sections:
Turnstiles 21-28 for the University of Wolverhampton Stand

ADMISSION INFO (2024/2025 PRICES)

Adult Seating: £24.00 – £29.00
Concessionary Seating: £21.00 – £25.00
Ages 18 to 20 Seating: £21.00
Ages 12 to 17 Seating: £15.00
Under-12s Seating: £5.00
Note: Discounts are available for advance bookings and savings from Family Tickets are available in some stands

FANS WITH DISABILITIES INFORMATION

Wheelchairs: 33 spaces in total for Home and Away fans in the a special section in the St. Francis Group Community Stand
Helpers: One helper admitted with each fan with disabilities
Prices: Normal prices apply for fans with disabilities. Helpers are admitted free of charge
Disabled Toilets: 5 available around the ground
A special Lounge for fans with disabilities is available
Contact: (01922) 651416   (Bookings are necessary)
Samantha Page (DLO) – sam.page@walsall.co.uk

Travelling Supporters' Information:
Routes: From All Parts: Exit the M6 at Junction 9 turning North towards Walsall onto the A461. After ¼ mile turn right into Wallows Lane and pass over the railway bridge. Then take the 1st right into Bescot Crescent and the ground is ½ mile along on the left adjacent to Bescot Railway Station.

F.A. Premier League 2023-2024 Season	Arsenal	Aston Villa	Bournemouth	Brentford	Brighton & Hove Albion	Burnley	Chelsea	Crystal Palace	Everton	Fulham	Liverpool	Luton Town	Manchester City	Manchester United	Newcastle United	Nottingham Forest	Sheffield United	Tottenham Hotspur	West Ham United	Wolverhampton Wanderers
Arsenal	■	0-2	3-0	2-1	2-0	3-1	5-0	5-0	2-1	2-2	3-1	2-0	1-0	3-1	4-1	2-1	5-0	2-2	0-2	2-1
Aston Villa	1-0	■	3-1	3-3	6-1	3-2	2-2	3-1	4-0	3-1	3-3	3-1	1-0	1-2	1-3	4-2	1-1	0-4	4-1	2-0
Bournemouth	0-4	2-2	■	1-2	3-0	2-1	0-0	1-0	2-1	3-0	0-4	4-3	0-1	2-2	2-0	1-1	2-2	0-2	1-1	1-2
Brentford	0-1	1-2	2-2	■	0-0	3-0	2-2	1-1	1-3	0-0	1-4	3-1	1-3	1-1	2-4	3-2	2-0	2-2	3-2	1-4
Brighton & Hove Albion	0-3	1-0	3-1	2-1	■	1-1	1-2	4-1	1-1	1-1	2-2	4-1	0-4	0-2	3-1	1-0	1-1	4-2	1-3	0-0
Burnley	0-5	1-3	0-2	2-1	1-1	■	1-4	0-2	0-2	2-2	0-2	1-1	0-3	0-1	1-4	1-2	5-0	2-5	1-2	1-1
Chelsea	2-2	0-1	2-1	0-2	3-2	2-2	■	2-1	6-0	1-0	1-1	3-0	4-4	4-3	3-2	0-1	2-0	2-0	5-0	2-4
Crystal Palace	0-1	5-0	0-2	3-1	1-1	3-0	1-3	■	2-3	0-0	1-2	1-1	2-4	4-0	2-0	0-0	3-2	1-2	5-2	3-2
Everton	0-1	0-0	3-0	1-0	1-1	1-0	2-0	1-1	■	0-1	2-0	1-2	1-3	0-3	3-0	2-0	1-0	2-2	1-3	0-1
Fulham	2-1	1-2	3-1	0-3	3-0	0-2	0-2	1-1	0-0	■	1-3	1-0	0-4	0-1	0-1	5-0	3-1	3-0	5-0	3-2
Liverpool	1-1	3-0	3-1	3-0	2-1	3-1	4-1	0-1	2-0	4-3	■	4-1	1-1	0-0	4-2	3-0	3-1	4-2	3-1	2-0
Luton Town	3-4	2-3	2-1	1-5	4-0	1-2	2-3	2-1	1-1	2-4	1-1	■	1-2	1-2	1-0	1-1	1-3	0-1	1-2	1-1
Manchester City	0-0	4-1	6-1	1-0	2-1	3-1	1-1	2-2	2-0	5-1	1-1	5-1	■	3-1	1-0	2-0	2-0	3-3	3-1	5-1
Manchester United	0-1	3-2	0-3	2-1	1-3	1-1	2-1	0-1	2-0	1-2	2-2	1-0	0-3	■	3-2	3-2	4-2	2-2	3-0	1-0
Newcastle United	1-0	5-1	2-2	1-0	1-1	2-0	4-1	4-0	1-1	3-0	1-2	4-4	2-3	1-0	■	1-3	5-1	4-0	4-3	3-0
Nottingham Forest	1-2	2-0	2-3	1-1	2-3	1-1	2-3	1-1	0-1	3-1	0-1	2-2	0-2	2-1	2-3	■	2-1	0-2	2-0	2-2
Sheffield United	0-6	0-5	1-3	1-0	0-5	1-4	2-2	0-1	2-2	3-3	0-2	2-3	1-2	1-2	0-8	1-3	■	0-3	2-2	2-1
Tottenham Hotspur	2-3	1-2	3-1	3-2	2-1	2-1	1-4	3-1	2-1	2-0	2-1	2-1	0-2	2-0	4-1	3-1	2-1	■	1-2	1-2
West Ham United	0-6	1-1	1-1	4-2	0-0	2-2	3-1	1-1	0-1	0-2	2-2	3-1	1-3	2-0	2-2	3-2	2-0	1-1	■	3-0
Wolverhampton Wanderers	0-2	1-1	0-1	0-2	1-4	1-0	2-1	1-3	3-0	2-1	1-3	2-1	2-1	3-4	2-2	1-1	1-0	2-1	1-2	■

EFL Championship 2023/2024 Season	Birmingham City	Blackburn Rovers	Bristol City	Cardiff City	Coventry City	Huddersfield Town	Hull City	Ipswich Town	Leeds United	Leicester City	Middlesbrough	Millwall	Norwich City	Plymouth Argyle	Preston North End	Queens Park Rangers	Rotherham United	Sheffield Wednesday	Southampton	Stoke City	Sunderland	Swansea City	Watford	West Bromwich Albion
Birmingham City		1-0	0-0	0-1	3-0	4-1	0-2	2-2	1-0	2-3	0-1	1-1	1-0	2-1	1-0	0-0	0-0	2-1	3-4	1-3	2-1	2-2	0-1	3-1
Blackburn Rovers	4-2		2-1	1-0	0-0	1-1	1-2	0-1	0-2	1-4	2-1	1-1	1-1	1-1	1-2	1-2	2-2	1-3	0-0	3-1	1-3	0-1	1-2	2-1
Bristol City	0-2	5-0		0-1	1-0	1-1	3-2	0-1	0-1	1-0	3-2	0-1	1-2	4-1	1-1	0-1	2-0	1-0	3-1	2-3	1-0	1-0	1-1	0-0
Cardiff City	0-1	0-0	2-0		3-2	1-0	1-3	2-1	0-3	0-2	1-4	1-0	2-3	2-2	0-2	1-2	2-0	2-1	2-1	2-1	0-2	2-0	1-1	0-1
Coventry City	2-0	1-0	2-2	1-2		1-1	2-3	1-2	2-1	3-1	3-0	2-1	1-1	1-0	0-3	1-2	5-0	2-0	1-1	0-0	0-0	2-2	3-3	0-2
Huddersfield Town	1-1	3-0	1-1	0-4	1-3		1-2	1-1	1-1	0-1	1-2	1-0	0-4	1-1	1-3	2-1	2-0	4-0	1-1	2-2	1-0	0-4	0-0	1-4
Hull City	1-1	3-2	1-1	3-0	1-1	1-0		3-3	0-0	2-2	2-2	1-0	1-2	1-1	1-0	3-0	4-1	4-2	1-2	0-2	0-1	0-1	1-2	1-1
Ipswich Town	3-1	4-3	3-2	3-2	2-1	2-0	3-0		3-4	1-1	1-1	3-1	2-2	3-2	4-2	0-0	4-3	6-0	3-2	2-0	2-1	3-2	0-0	2-2
Leeds United	3-0	0-1	2-1	2-2	1-1	4-1	3-1	4-0		3-1	3-2	2-0	1-0	2-1	2-1	1-0	3-0	0-0	1-2	1-0	0-0	3-1	3-0	1-1
Leicester City	2-1	0-2	1-0	2-1	2-1	4-1	0-1	1-1	0-1		1-2	3-2	3-1	4-0	3-0	1-2	3-0	2-0	5-0	2-0	1-0	3-1	2-0	2-1
Middlesbrough	1-0	0-0	1-2	2-0	1-3	1-1	1-2	0-2	3-4	1-0		0-1	3-1	0-2	4-0	0-2	1-1	2-0	2-1	0-2	1-1	2-0	3-1	1-0
Millwall	1-0	1-2	0-1	3-1	0-3	1-1	2-2	0-4	0-3	1-0	1-3		1-0	1-0	1-1	2-0	3-0	0-2	0-1	1-0	1-1	0-3	1-0	1-1
Norwich City	2-0	1-3	1-1	4-1	2-1	2-0	2-1	1-0	2-3	0-2	1-2	3-1		2-1	0-0	1-0	5-0	3-1	1-1	1-0	1-0	2-2	4-2	2-0
Plymouth Argyle	3-3	3-0	0-1	3-1	2-2	3-1	1-0	0-2	0-2	1-0	3-3	0-2	6-2		0-1	1-1	3-2	3-0	1-2	2-1	2-0	1-3	3-3	0-3
Preston North End	2-1	2-2	2-0	1-2	3-2	4-1	0-0	3-2	2-1	0-3	2-1	1-1	0-1	2-1		0-2	3-0	0-1	2-2	1-2	2-1	2-1	1-5	0-4
Queens Park Rangers	2-1	0-4	0-0	1-2	1-3	1-1	2-0	0-1	4-0	1-2	0-2	2-0	2-2	0-0	1-0		2-1	0-2	0-1	4-2	1-3	1-1	1-2	2-2
Rotherham United	0-0	2-2	1-2	5-2	2-0	0-0	1-2	2-2	1-1	1-2	1-0	2-1	2-1	0-1	1-1	1-1		0-1	0-2	0-1	1-1	1-2	0-1	0-2
Sheffield Wednesday	2-0	3-1	2-1	1-2	1-2	0-0	3-1	0-1	0-2	1-1	1-1	0-4	2-2	1-0	0-1	2-1	2-0		1-2	1-1	0-3	1-1	0-0	3-0
Southampton	3-1	4-0	1-0	2-0	2-1	5-3	1-2	0-1	3-1	1-4	1-1	1-2	4-4	2-1	3-0	2-1	1-1	4-0		0-1	4-2	5-0	3-2	2-1
Stoke City	1-2	0-3	4-0	0-0	0-1	1-1	1-3	0-0	1-0	0-5	2-0	0-0	0-3	3-0	0-2	1-0	4-1	0-1	0-1		2-1	1-1	1-0	2-2
Sunderland	3-1	1-5	0-0	0-1	0-3	1-2	0-1	1-2	1-0	0-1	0-4	0-1	3-1	3-1	2-0	0-0	2-1	0-2	5-0	3-1		1-2	2-0	2-1
Swansea City	1-1	2-1	1-2	2-0	1-1	1-1	2-2	1-2	0-4	1-3	1-2	0-1	2-1	0-1	2-1	0-1	1-0	3-0	1-3	3-0	0-0		0-1	1-0
Watford	2-0	0-1	1-4	0-1	1-2	1-2	0-0	1-2	2-2	1-2	2-3	2-2	3-2	0-0	0-0	4-0	5-0	1-0	1-1	1-1	1-0	1-1		2-2
West Bromwich Albion	1-0	4-1	2-0	2-0	2-1	1-2	3-1	2-0	1-0	1-2	4-2	0-0	1-0	0-0	3-0	2-0	2-0	1-0	0-2	1-1	0-1	3-2	2-2	

EFL League One 2023-2024 Season

	Barnsley	Blackpool	Bolton Wanderers	Bristol City	Burton Albion	Cambridge United	Carlisle United	Charlton Athletic	Cheltenham Town	Derby County	Exeter City	Fleetwood Town	Leyton Orient	Lincoln City	Northampton Town	Oxford United	Peterborough United	Portsmouth	Port Vale	Reading	Shrewsbury Town	Stevenage	Wigan Athletic	Wycombe Wanderers
Barnsley		0-1	2-2	2-1	2-0	0-2	2-1	1-1	0-0	2-1	1-2	2-2	2-1	1-5	1-1	1-3	1-3	2-3	7-0	2-2	3-0	2-1	1-1	1-0
Blackpool	3-2		4-1	3-1	2-0	1-0	3-0	1-1	3-2	1-3	2-0	1-0	0-0	2-0	1-2	1-1	2-4	0-0	0-0	4-1	4-0	3-0	2-1	0-0
Bolton Wanderers	1-1	1-0		1-2	1-0	2-0	1-3	3-3	1-0	2-1	7-0	3-1	3-2	3-0	2-1	5-0	1-1	1-1	2-0	5-2	2-2	3-2	0-4	2-1
Bristol Rovers	1-1	1-2	0-2		1-2	1-0	2-1	2-1	1-1	0-3	0-1	0-2	1-1	1-1	2-1	3-1	0-2	2-1	3-0	0-2	0-0	1-1	4-1	1-2
Burton Albion	1-3	1-0	1-1	4-1		2-1	0-1	2-0	1-2	0-3	0-1	1-1	0-0	0-1	0-2	0-4	1-3	0-2	0-1	3-2	1-0	1-2	2-1	1-1
Cambridge United	0-4	2-1	1-2	2-0	0-0		1-0	1-1	0-1	0-1	2-0	2-1	0-2	0-3	1-1	2-0	0-1	0-0	1-1	1-0	1-1	1-2	3-1	1-1
Carlisle United	2-3	0-1	1-4	0-1	2-1	0-4		1-1	0-1	0-2	0-2	1-1	0-1	1-3	2-2	1-3	1-1	0-1	2-1	1-3	2-0	2-2	1-1	1-3
Charlton Athletic	2-1	2-2	0-2	1-2	1-1	2-2	3-2		2-1	0-1	4-1	2-1	1-0	1-1	2-3	1-2	1-2	0-0	2-3	4-0	1-1	0-0	2-2	3-1
Cheltenham Town	0-2	2-0	0-3	1-3	0-0	1-0	0-1	1-3		1-1	1-2	0-2	1-2	1-2	0-1	2-0	2-0	2-1	3-2	2-2	2-0	0-3	1-1	1-3
Derby County	3-0	1-0	1-0	2-1	3-2	0-0	2-0	1-2	2-1		2-0	1-0	3-0	3-1	4-0	1-2	2-3	1-1	3-0	2-1	1-1	1-0	1-2	1-1
Exeter City	0-1	0-0	2-2	0-1	1-0	0-0	2-1	1-1	1-0	0-3		1-1	1-2	1-0	0-2	1-2	2-1	0-0	0-1	2-1	0-0	1-0	0-2	1-0
Fleetwood Town	1-2	3-3	0-2	0-0	3-0	0-2	1-1	1-0	1-2	1-3	3-0		1-0	0-1	2-0	0-3	0-1	3-0	1-1	0-3			4-2	1-4
Leyton Orient	1-1	1-0	1-0	0-1	1-2	2-0	3-2	1-0	3-1	0-3	2-2	0-1		0-1	4-3	2-3	1-2	0-4	0-0	2-1	1-0	0-3	1-1	0-0
Lincoln City	2-2	3-0	0-1	5-0	0-1	6-0	1-1	3-1	2-0	0-0	1-0	2-1	1-0		1-2	0-2	0-0	2-1	1-1	1-1	3-0	0-0	1-2	3-0
Northampton Town	1-2	0-1	1-1	3-1	2-0	2-1	2-0	1-1	1-0	1-2	3-0	2-2	2-2			2-1	1-0	0-3	2-0	3-1	0-2	0-1	1-1	0-1
Oxford United	0-1	1-1	0-0	2-1	3-0	2-1	1-0	2-1	2-3	3-0	4-0	1-2	0-1	2-2			5-0	2-2	1-2	1-1	3-0	1-1	4-2	2-2
Peterborough United	2-2	1-2	3-3	2-0	4-0	5-0	1-3	1-0	3-0	2-4	2-1	4-1	1-1	2-0	5-1	3-0		0-1	3-0	2-2	2-1	3-1	2-3	2-2
Portsmouth	3-2	0-4	2-0	1-1	2-1	3-1	1-0	2-2	0-0	2-2	1-0	1-1	0-3	2-1	4-1	2-1	3-1		2-0	4-1	3-1	2-1	1-2	2-1
Port Vale	2-3	3-0	0-1	2-0	2-3	0-0	1-0	3-3	1-2	0-1	2-4	2-2	0-1	1-0	0-2	1-0	0-1	0-1		1-0	1-2	2-2	3-2	1-2
Reading	1-3	3-2	2-1	1-1	0-0	4-0	5-1	2-0	1-0	1-0	3-2	1-2	1-1	1-1	1-0	1-1	0-1	2-3	2-0		2-3	2-0	2-0	2-1
Shrewsbury Town	1-1	0-2	0-2	0-2	2-1	1-2	1-0	0-0	1-0	1-0	0-3	3-1	1-3	0-1	1-0	1-1	1-2	0-3	2-1	3-2		0-1	0-1	0-2
Stevenage	2-1	1-0	0-0	2-3	1-2	1-0	2-2	1-1	2-1	3-1	1-1	0-0	0-1	1-0	3-0	1-3	2-2	0-0	0-0	0-1	2-0		1-0	1-0
Wigan Athletic	0-2	1-0	1-0	2-0	1-1	2-1	2-0	2-3	1-1	0-1	1-2	3-0	1-0	0-0	2-1	2-0	2-1	1-2	0-0	1-0	2-0	2-3		1-0
Wycombe Wanderers	2-4	2-0	2-4	3-2	0-0	0-0	2-0	1-0	2-0	0-0	0-3	2-2	3-2	1-1	2-0	0-0	5-2	1-3	1-1	1-2	0-1	0-1	1-0	

EFL League Two 2023-2024 Season	Accrington Stanley	AFC Wimbledon	Barrow	Bradford City	Colchester United	Crawley Town	Crewe Alexandra	Doncaster Rovers	Forest Green Rovers	Gillingham	Grimsby Town	Harrogate Town	Mansfield Town	MK Dons	Morecambe	Newport County	Notts County	Salford City	Stockport County	Sutton United	Swindon Town	Tranmere Rovers	Walsall	Wrexham
Accrington Stanley		2-0	1-1	0-3	0-1	0-1	0-0	0-0	2-1	1-2	0-0	2-1	0-3	1-0	1-2	3-0	2-2	3-0	1-3	4-1	3-4	4-1	2-1	2-0
AFC Wimbledon	2-4		2-0	0-1	5-3	0-1	2-2	2-0	1-1	2-0	0-0	1-1	2-1	1-0	1-1	0-2	4-2	1-0	1-2	0-1	4-0	4-1	5-1	1-1
Barrow	1-1	0-0		1-2	2-0	1-0	1-3	3-2	1-2	2-0	3-1	0-0	1-1	1-0	1-0	1-0	1-1	0-0	2-2	2-1	0-2	1-0	2-0	1-1
Bradford City	1-0	0-0	1-2		2-1	2-4	1-0	1-1	0-2	1-0	1-1	1-1	1-5	4-0	2-2	4-1	0-3	1-1	0-0	1-0	1-0	2-0	1-3	1-1
Colchester United	1-1	0-2	1-4	1-1		1-2	1-1	1-4	3-3	0-1	2-0	1-2	1-1	2-3	1-3	2-1	5-4	2-1	1-2	1-1	3-1	2-0	1-1	1-2
Crawley Town	3-1	1-2	1-1	1-0	2-3		2-4	0-2	2-0	0-1	2-0	2-1	1-3	2-1	1-2	4-1	2-1	0-1	1-1	3-0	3-1	3-2	1-1	0-1
Crewe Alexandra	3-3	1-1	1-3	1-0	2-1	1-0		3-2	0-3	2-0	0-3	0-0	2-2	3-1	2-3	4-2	1-0	2-3	0-2	1-0	2-1	2-0	2-2	0-3
Doncaster Rovers	4-0	1-0	4-2	1-3	3-1	2-0	2-0		2-0	2-1	1-0	0-1	2-2	3-0	0-5	0-1	1-3	0-3	1-5	4-1	0-0	2-1	2-1	1-0
Forest Green Rovers	0-1	1-1	0-2	0-3	5-0	2-1	1-4	1-2		0-0	2-2	0-2	0-4	0-2	1-2	0-3	1-0	0-2	0-3	0-1	1-2	1-0	2-0	1-1
Gillingham	1-0	1-0	3-0	0-2	0-3	0-2	0-0	2-2	1-1		1-1	1-0	1-1	2-1	2-1	0-2	1-2	3-1	0-0	1-0	2-2	1-1	1-1	1-0
Grimsby Town	0-2	0-0	2-1	1-1	2-3	2-3	2-1	1-5	1-0	2-0		1-2	1-1	1-0	3-2	1-0	5-5	2-0	1-3	1-1	2-0	1-2	1-6	1-3
Harrogate Town	2-1	0-1	0-1	3-0	1-0	1-2	0-1	3-1	0-1	5-1	1-0		1-4	3-5	2-0	1-4	3-1	3-2	1-3	2-2	1-1	0-2	0-2	2-2
Mansfield Town	2-1	0-1	1-0	0-0	1-1	1-4	0-1	1-1	1-0	2-1	2-0	9-2		1-2	3-0	2-0	1-0	5-1	3-2	1-1	3-2	2-2	2-1	0-0
Milton Keynes Dons	2-1	3-1	2-2	4-1	1-0	2-0	3-1	2-1	2-0	2-1	1-1	0-1	1-4		1-2	3-0	1-1	3-1	1-2	4-4	3-2	1-0	5-0	1-1
Morecambe	1-1	4-1	2-1	3-0	0-1	1-0	0-1	0-3	1-2	2-3	1-1	2-2	1-1	1-3		1-2	0-0	1-0	1-1	1-0	2-2	1-0	2-1	1-3
Newport County	1-3	2-2	1-1	1-4	2-1	0-4	1-1	4-0	4-2	1-0	1-1	1-2	0-1	0-0	5-3		1-3	0-1	2-1	3-1	2-1	1-2	3-3	1-0
Notts County	3-1	0-2	1-1	4-2	1-0	3-1	1-3	3-0	4-3	1-3	3-2	3-0	1-4	3-3	5-0	3-0		1-2	2-5	3-4	3-1	2-1	1-2	0-2
Salford City	1-2	0-0	5-3	1-2	1-1	1-1	4-2	2-2	2-2	0-2	0-3	2-2	1-2	2-4	3-1	2-1	0-2		2-2	1-2	2-2	1-5	1-2	3-1
Stockport County	4-2	1-0	1-0	1-1	2-0	3-3	1-3	1-0	2-0	0-1	3-2	1-1	0-2	5-0	2-0	1-0	2-1	0-0		8-0	0-0	2-0	3-1	5-0
Sutton United	3-1	0-3	2-2	2-1	1-1	2-2	1-1	1-1	0-1	0-1	1-1	1-2	0-2	1-1	2-3	1-1	5-1	0-2	1-3		3-1	1-1	4-0	1-1
Swindon Town	1-2	3-2	0-3	2-0	2-2	6-0	2-2	1-2	2-1	0-1	2-1	1-1	2-1	1-2	3-3	2-0	2-1	1-1	2-4	5-3		3-1	2-0	0-1
Tranmere Rovers	2-0	3-2	1-2	2-1	1-1	1-3	0-0	1-2	3-0	3-1	2-2	3-0	2-1	1-2	2-3	2-1	4-2	3-4	4-0	1-0	2-1		1-3	0-1
Walsall	2-1	1-3	1-1	2-3	1-0	1-1	2-0	3-1	0-0	4-1	1-1	0-1	2-1	0-0	3-0	0-3	1-3	2-1	2-1	1-1	2-1	1-0		3-1
Wrexham	4-0	2-0	4-1	0-1	2-1	4-1	3-3	2-1	6-0	2-0	3-0	0-0	2-0	3-5	6-0	2-0	1-0	3-2	2-1	2-1	5-5	0-1	4-2	

Premier League

Season 2023/2024

	P	W	D	L	F	A	Pts
MANCHESTER CITY	38	28	7	3	96	34	91
Arsenal	38	28	5	5	91	29	89
Liverpool	38	24	10	4	86	41	82
Aston Villa	38	20	8	10	76	61	68
Tottenham Hotspur	38	20	6	12	74	61	66
Chelsea	38	18	9	11	77	63	63
Newcastle United	38	18	6	14	85	62	60
Manchester United	38	18	6	14	57	58	60
West Ham United	38	14	10	14	60	74	52
Crystal Palace	38	13	10	15	57	58	49
Brighton & Hove Albion	38	12	12	14	55	62	48
Bournemouth	38	13	9	16	54	67	48
Fulham	38	13	8	17	55	61	47
Wolverhampton Wanderers	38	13	7	18	50	65	46
Everton	38	13	9	16	40	51	40
Brentford	38	10	9	19	56	65	39
Nottingham Forest	38	9	9	20	49	67	32
Luton Town	*38*	*6*	*8*	*24*	*52*	*85*	*26*
Burnley	*38*	*5*	*9*	*24*	*41*	*78*	*24*
Sheffield United	*38*	*3*	*7*	*28*	*35*	*104*	*16*

Everton had 8 points deducted after breaching the league's profitability and sustainability rules.
The deduction was originally 10 points but this was reduced to six on appeal. The club then had an additional two points deducted for further breaches.
Nottingham Forest had 4 points deducted for the breaching profitability and sustainability rules.

Champions: Manchester City

Relegated: Luton Town, Burnley and Sheffield United

EFL Championship

Season 2023/2024

	P	W	D	L	F	A	Pts
Leicester City	46	31	4	11	89	41	97
Ipswich Town	46	28	12	6	92	57	96
Leeds United	46	27	9	10	81	43	90
Southampton	46	26	9	11	87	63	87
West Bromwich Albion	46	21	12	13	70	47	75
Norwich City	46	21	10	15	79	64	73
Hull City	46	19	13	14	68	60	70
Middlesbrough	46	20	9	17	71	62	69
Coventry City	46	17	13	16	70	59	64
Preston North End	46	18	9	19	56	67	63
Bristol City	46	17	11	18	53	51	62
Cardiff City	46	19	5	22	53	70	62
Millwall	46	16	11	19	45	55	59
Swansea City	46	15	12	19	59	65	57
Watford	46	13	17	16	61	61	56
Sunderland	46	16	8	22	52	54	56
Stoke City	46	15	11	20	49	60	56
Queens Park Rangers	46	15	11	20	47	58	56
Blackburn Rovers	46	14	11	21	60	74	53
Sheffield Wednesday	46	15	8	23	44	68	53
Plymouth Argyle	46	13	12	21	59	70	51
Birmingham City	*46*	*13*	*11*	*22*	*50*	*65*	*50*
Huddersfield Town	*46*	*9*	*18*	*19*	*48*	*77*	*45*
Rotherham United	*46*	*5*	*12*	*29*	*37*	*89*	*27*

Promotion Play-offs

Norwich City 0	Leeds United 0
West Bromwich Albion 0	Southampton 0

Leeds United 0	Norwich City 4

Norwich City won 4-0 on aggregate.

Southampton 3	West Bromwich Albion 1

Southampton won 3-1 on aggregate.

Norwich City 0	Southampton 1

Promoted: Leicester City, Ipswich Town and Southampton

Relegated: Birmingham City, Huddersfield Town and Rotherham United

EFL League One

Season 2023/2024

Portsmouth	46	28	13	5	78	41	97
Derby County	46	28	8	10	78	37	92
Bolton Wanderers	46	25	12	9	86	51	87
Peterborough United	46	25	9	12	89	61	84
Oxford United	46	22	11	13	79	56	77
Barnsley	46	21	13	12	82	64	76
Lincoln City	46	20	14	12	65	40	74
Blackpool	46	21	10	15	65	48	73
Stevenage	46	19	14	13	57	46	71
Wycombe Wanderers	46	17	14	15	60	55	65
Leyton Orient	46	18	11	17	53	55	65
Wigan Athletic	46	20	10	16	63	56	62
Exeter City	46	17	10	19	46	61	61
Northampton Town	46	17	9	20	57	66	60
Bristol Rovers	46	16	9	21	52	68	57
Charlton Athletic	46	11	20	15	64	65	53
Reading	46	16	11	19	68	70	53
Cambridge United	46	12	12	22	39	61	48
Shrewsbury Town	46	13	9	24	35	67	48
Burton Albion	46	12	10	24	39	67	46
Cheltenham Town	*46*	*12*	*8*	*26*	*41*	*65*	*44*
Fleetwood Town	*46*	*10*	*13*	*23*	*49*	*72*	*43*
Port Vale	*46*	*10*	*11*	*25*	*41*	*74*	*41*
Carlisle United	*46*	*7*	*9*	*30*	*41*	*81*	*30*

Wigan Athletic had a total of 8 points deducted for failing to pay players and staff on time and missing a deadline to deposit an amount equalling 125% of its monthly wage bill.

Reading had 4 points deducted after failing to pay players on time and a further 2 points deducted for late payments to HMRC.

Promotion Play-offs

Barnsley	1	Bolton Wanderers	3
Oxford United	1	Peterborough United	0

Bolton Wanderers	2	Barnsley	3

Bolton Wanderers won 5-4 on aggregate.

Peterborough United	1	Oxford United	1

Oxford United won 2-1 on aggregate.

Bolton Wanderers	0	Oxford United	2

Promoted: Portsmouth, Derby County and Oxford United

Relegated: Cheltenham Town, Fleetwood Town, Port Vale and Carlisle United

EFL League Two

Season 2023/2024

Stockport County	46	27	11	8	96	48	92
Wrexham	46	26	10	10	89	52	88
Mansfield Town	46	24	14	8	90	47	86
Milton Keynes Dons	46	23	9	14	83	68	78
Doncaster Rovers	46	21	8	17	73	68	71
Crewe Alexandra	46	19	14	13	69	65	71
Crawley Town	**46**	**21**	**7**	**18**	**73**	**67**	**70**
Barrow	46	18	15	13	62	56	69
Bradford City	46	19	12	15	61	59	69
AFC Wimbledon	46	17	14	15	64	51	65
Walsall	46	18	11	17	69	73	65
Gillingham	46	18	10	18	46	57	64
Harrogate Town	46	17	12	17	60	69	63
Notts County	46	18	7	21	89	86	61
Morecambe	46	17	10	19	67	81	58
Tranmere Rovers	46	17	6	23	67	70	57
Accrington Stanley	46	16	9	21	63	71	57
Newport County	46	16	7	23	62	76	55
Swindon Town	46	14	12	20	77	83	54
Salford City	46	13	12	21	66	82	51
Grimsby Town	46	11	16	19	57	74	49
Colchester United	46	11	12	23	59	80	45
Sutton United	*46*	*9*	*15*	*22*	*59*	*84*	*42*
Forest Green Rovers	*46*	*11*	*9*	*26*	*44*	*78*	*42*

Morecambe had 3 points deducted after failing to pay players and staff on time.

Promotion Play-offs

Crewe Alexandra	0	Doncaster Rovers	2
Crawley Town	3	Milton Keynes Dons	0

Doncaster Rovers	2	Crewe Alexandra	0 (aet)

Aggregate 2-2. Crewe Alexandra won 4-3 on penalties.

Milton Keynes Dons	1	Crawley Town	5

Crawley Town won 8-1 on aggregate.

Crewe Alexandra	0	Crawley Town	2

Promoted: Stockport County, Wrexham, Mansfield Town and Crawley Town

Relegated: Sutton United and Forest Green Rovers

F.A. Cup 2023/2024

Round 1	Crewe Alexandra	2	Derby County	2	
Round 1	Charlton Athletic	1	Cray Valley Paper Mills	1	
Round 1	Chesterfield	1	Portsmouth	0	
Round 1	Kidderminster Harriers	1	Fleetwood	2	
Round 1	Slough	1	Grimsby Town	1	
Round 1	Northampton Town	1	Barrow	3	
Round 1	AFC Wimbledon	5	Cheltenham Town	1	
Round 1	Alfreton Town	2	Worthing	0	
Round 1	Bolton Wanderers	4	Solihull Moors	0	
Round 1	Bradford City	1	Wycombe Wanderers	2	
Round 1	Bristol Rovers	7	Whitby	2	
Round 1	Cambridge United	2	Bracknell Town	1	
Round 1	Chesham	0	Maidstone United	2	
Round 1	Chester FC	0	York City	0	
Round 1	Curzon Ashton	0	Barnet	1	
Round 1	Doncaster Rovers	2	Accrington Stanley	2	
Round 1	Eastleigh	5	Boreham Wood	1	
Round 1	Exeter City	0	Wigan Athletic	2	
Round 1	Hereford	0	Gillingham	2	
Round 1	Leyton Orient	3	Carlisle United	1	
Round 1	Lincoln City	1	Morecambe	2	
Round 1	Marine	1	Harrogate	5	
Round 1	Newport County	2	Oldham Athletic	0	
Round 1	Notts County	3	Crawley Town	2	
Round 1	Oxford United	2	Maidenhead United	0	
Round 1	Peterborough United	2	Salford City	2	
Round 1	Port Vale	0	Burton Albion	0	
Round 1	Ramsgate	2	Woking	1	
Round 1	Reading	3	Milton Keynes Dons	2	
Round 1	Scarborough Athletic	1	Forest Green Rovers	1	
Round 1	Shrewsbury Town	3	Colchester United	2	
Round 1	Stevenage	4	Tranmere Rovers	3	
Round 1	Stockport County	5	Worksop Town	1	
Round 1	Sutton United	2	AFC Fylde	1	
Round 1	Swindon Town	4	Aldershot Town	7	
Round 1	Yeovil Town	3	Gateshead	2	
Round 1	Bromley	0	Blackpool	2	
Round 1	Mansfield Town	1	Wrexham	2	
Round 1	Barnsley	3	Horsham	3	
Round 1	Sheppey United	1	Walsall	4	
Replay	Accrington Stanley	1	Doncaster Rovers	2	(aet)
Replay	Burton Albion	0	Port Vale	2	
Replay	Cray Valley Paper Mills	1	Charlton Athletic	6	
Replay	Derby County	1	Crewe Alexandra	3	
Replay	Forest Green Rovers	5	Scarborough Athletic	2	
	A replay was ordered after Forest Green Rovers fielded an ineligible player.				
Replay	Grimsby Town	7	Slough	2	
Replay	Horsham	0	Barnsley	3	
Replay	Salford City	4	Peterborough United	4	(aet)
	Peterborough United won 5-4 on penalties.				
Replay	York City	2	Chester FC	1	
Replay	Scarborough Athletic	2	Forest Green Rovers	4	

Round 2	AFC Wimbledon	5	Ramsgate	0	
Round 2	Aldershot Town	2	Stockport County	2	
Round 2	Alfreton Town	0	Walsall	0	
Round 2	Blackpool	3	Forest Green Rovers	0	
Round 2	Bolton Wanderers	5	Harrogate	1	
Round 2	Cambridge United	4	Fleetwood	0	
Round 2	Chesterfield	1	Leyton Orient	0	
Round 2	Eastleigh	2	Reading	1	
Round 2	Gillingham	2	Charlton Athletic	0	
Round 2	Maidstone United	2	Barrow	1	
Round 2	Newport County	1	Barnet	1	
Round 2	Notts County	2	Shrewsbury Town	3	
Round 2	Oxford United	2	Grimsby Town	0	
Round 2	Peterborough United	2	Doncaster Rovers	1	
Round 2	Stevenage	1	Port Vale	1	
Round 2	Sutton United	3	Horsham	0	
Round 2	Wrexham	3	Yeovil Town	0	
Round 2	Wycombe Wanderers	0	Morecambe	2	
Round 2	York City	0	Wigan Athletic	1	
Round 2	Crewe Alexandra	2	Bristol Rovers	4	
Replay	Stockport County	0	Aldershot Town	1	
Replay	Barnet	1	Newport County	4	
Replay	Port Vale	3	Stevenage	3	(aet)
	Stevenage won 4-3 on penalties.				
Replay	Walsall	1	Alfreton Town	0	
Round 3	AFC Wimbledon	1	Ipswich Town	3	
Round 3	Arsenal	0	Liverpool	2	
Round 3	Blackburn Rovers	5	Cambridge United	2	
Round 3	Brentford	1	Wolverhampton Wanderers	1	
Round 3	Chelsea	4	Preston North End	0	
Round 3	Coventry City	6	Oxford United	2	
Round 3	Crystal Palace	0	Everton	0	
Round 3	Fulham	1	Rotherham United	0	
Round 3	Gillingham	0	Sheffield United	4	
Round 3	Hull City	1	Birmingham City	1	
Round 3	Luton Town	0	Bolton Wanderers	0	
Round 3	Maidstone United	1	Stevenage	0	
Round 3	Manchester City	5	Huddersfield Town	0	
Round 3	Middlesbrough	0	Aston Villa	1	
Round 3	Millwall	2	Leicester City	3	
Round 3	Newport County	1	Eastleigh	1	
Round 3	Norwich City	1	Bristol Rovers	1	
Round 3	Nottingham Forest	2	Blackpool	2	
Round 3	Peterborough United	0	Leeds United	3	
Round 3	Plymouth Argyle	3	Sutton United	1	
Round 3	Queen's Park Rangers	2	Bournemouth	3	
Round 3	Sheffield Wednesday	4	Cardiff City	0	
Round 3	Shrewsbury Town	0	Wrexham	1	
Round 3	Southampton	4	Walsall	0	
Round 3	Stoke City	2	Brighton & Hove Albion	4	
Round 3	Sunderland	0	Newcastle United	3	
Round 3	Swansea City	2	Morecambe	0	
Round 3	Tottenham Hotspur	1	Burnley	0	
Round 3	Watford	2	Chesterfield	1	
Round 3	West Bromwich Albion	4	Aldershot Town	1	
Round 3	West Ham United	1	Bristol City	1	
Round 3	Wigan Athletic	0	Manchester United	2	

Replay	Blackpool	2	Nottingham Forest	3	(aet)
Replay	Bristol Rovers	1	Norwich City	3	
Replay	Everton	1	Crystal Palace	0	
Replay	Wolverhampton Wanderers	3	Brentford	2	(aet)
Replay	Birmingham City	2	Hull City	1	
Replay	Bolton Wanderers	1	Luton Town	2	
Replay	Bristol City	1	West Ham United	0	
Replay	Eastleigh	1	Newport County	3	
Round 4	Bournemouth	5	Swansea City	0	
Round 4	Tottenham Hotspur	0	Manchester City	1	
Round 4	Sheffield Wednesday	1	Coventry City	1	
Round 4	Chelsea	0	Aston Villa	0	
Round 4	Bristol City	0	Nottingham Forest	0	
Round 4	Ipswich Town	1	Maidstone United	2	
Round 4	Everton	1	Luton Town	2	
Round 4	Leeds United	1	Plymouth Argyle	1	
Round 4	Leicester City	3	Birmingham City	0	
Round 4	Sheffield United	2	Brighton & Hove Albion	5	
Round 4	Fulham	0	Newcastle United	2	
Round 4	West Bromwich Albion	0	Wolverhampton Wanderers	2	
Round 4	Watford	1	Southampton	1	
Round 4	Liverpool	5	Norwich City	2	
Round 4	Newport County	2	Manchester United	4	
Round 4	Blackburn Rovers	4	Wrexham	1	
Replay	Nottingham Forest	1	Bristol City	1	(aet)
	Nottingham Forest won 5-3 on penalties.				
Replay	Plymouth Argyle	1	Leeds United	4	(aet)
Replay	Southampton	3	Watford	0	
Replay	Coventry City	4	Sheffield Wednesday	1	
Replay	Aston Villa	1	Chelsea	3	
Round 5	Coventry City	5	Maidstone United	0	
Round 5	Chelsea	3	Leeds United	2	
Round 5	Nottingham Forest	0	Manchester United	1	
Round 5	Wolverhampton Wanderers	1	Brighton & Hove Albion	0	
Round 5	Liverpool	3	Southampton	0	
Round 5	Bournemouth	0	Leicester City	1	(aet)
Round 5	Blackburn Rovers	1	Newcastle United	1	(aet)
	Newcastle United won 4-3 on penalties.				
Round 5	Luton Town	2	Manchester City	6	
Round 6	Wolverhampton Wanderers	2	Coventry City	3	
Round 6	Manchester City	2	Newcastle United	0	
Round 6	Chelsea	4	Leicester City	2	
Round 6	Manchester United	4	Liverpool	3	(aet)
Semi-final	Manchester City	1	Chelsea	0	
Semi-final	Manchester United	3	Coventry City	3	(aet)
	Manchester United won 4-2 on penalties.				
FINAL	Manchester United	2	Manchester City	1	

EFL Cup 2023/2024

Round 1	Accrington Stanley	1	Bradford City	1
	Bradford City won 4-1 on penalties.			
Round 1	AFC Wimbledon	2	Coventry City	1
Round 1	Barnsley	2	Tranmere Rovers	2
	Tranmere Rovers won 7-6 on penalties.			
Round 1	Blackburn Rovers	4	Walsall	3
Round 1	Bolton Wanderers	1	Barrow	0
Round 1	Bristol City	5	Oxford United	1
Round 1	Cardiff City	2	Colchester United	2
	Cardiff City won 3-0 on penalties.			
Round 1	Cheltenham Town	0	Birmingham City	2
Round 1	Derby County	0	Blackpool	2
Round 1	Exeter City	2	Crawley Town	1
Round 1	Forest Green Rovers	1	Portsmouth	3
Round 1	Gillingham	3	Southampton	1
Round 1	Harrogate Town	1	Carlisle United	0
Round 1	Huddersfield Town	2	Middlesbrough	3
Round 1	Hull City	1	Doncaster Rovers	2
Round 1	Ipswich Town	2	Bristol Rovers	0
Round 1	Leeds United	2	Shrewsbury Town	1
Round 1	Mansfield Town	2	Grimsby Town	0
Round 1	Millwall	0	Reading	4
Round 1	Milton Keynes Dons	0	Wycombe Wanderers	2
Round 1	Newport County	3	Charlton Athletic	1
Round 1	Notts County	0	Lincoln City	2
Round 1	Peterborough United	1	Swindon Town	1
	Peterborough United won 4-1 on penalties.			
Round 1	Plymouth Argyle	2	Leyton Orient	0
Round 1	Port Vale	3	Fleetwood Town	2
Round 1	Preston North End	2	Salford City	2
	Salford City won 4-2 on penalties.			
Round 1	Queens Park Rangers	0	Norwich City	1
Round 1	Rotherham United	1	Morecambe	1
	Rotherham United won 4-2 on penalties.			
Round 1	Sheffield Wednesday	1	Stockport County	1
	Sheffield Wednesday won 4-1 on penalties.			
Round 1	Stevenage	1	Watford	1
	Stevenage won 4-3 on penalties.			
Round 1	Stoke City	2	West Bromwich Albion	1
Round 1	Sunderland	1	Crewe Alexandra	1
	Crewe Alexandra won 5-3 on penalties.			
Round 1	Sutton United	2	Cambridge United	2
	Sutton United won 6-5 on penalties.			
Round 1	Swansea City	3	Northampton Town	0
Round 1	Wrexham	0	Wigan Athletic	0
	Wrexham won 4-2 on penalties.			
Round 1	Burton Albion	0	Leicester City	2
Round 2	Birmingham City	1	Cardiff City	3
Round 2	Bolton Wanderers	1	Middlesbrough	3
Round 2	Bristol City	0	Norwich City	1

Round 2	Exeter City	1	Stevenage	1
	Exeter City won 5-3 on penalties.			
Round 2	Fulham	1	Tottenham Hotspur	1
	Fulham won 5-3 on penalties.			
Round 2	Luton Town	3	Gillingham	2
Round 2	Newport County	1	Brentford	1
	Brentford won 3-0 on penalties.			
Round 2	Plymouth Argyle	2	Crystal Palace	4
Round 2	Port Vale	0	Crewe Alexandra	0
	Port Vale won 2-0 on penalties.			
Round 2	Portsmouth	1	Peterborough United	1
	Peterborough United won 5-4 on penalties.			
Round 2	Reading	2	Ipswich Town	2
	Ipswich Town won 3-1 on penalties.			
Round 2	Salford City	1	Leeds United	1
	Salford City won 9-8 on penalties.			
Round 2	Sheffield Wednesday	1	Mansfield Town	1
	Mansfield Town won 5-4 on penalties.			
Round 2	Stoke City	6	Rotherham United	1
Round 2	Swansea City	2	Bournemouth	3
Round 2	Tranmere Rovers	0	Leicester City	2
Round 2	Wolverhampton Wanderers	5	Blackpool	0
Round 2	Wrexham	1	Bradford City	1
	Bradford City won 4-3 on penalties.			
Round 2	Wycombe Wanderers	0	Sutton United	1
Round 2	Chelsea	2	AFC Wimbledon	1
Round 2	Doncaster Rovers	1	Everton	2
Round 2	Harrogate Town	0	Blackburn Rovers	8
Round 2	Nottingham Forest	0	Burnley	1
Round 2	Sheffield United	0	Lincoln City	0
	Lincoln City won 3-2 on penalties.			
Round 3	Bradford City	0	Middlesbrough	2
Round 3	Exeter City	1	Luton Town	0
Round 3	Ipswich Town	3	Wolverhampton Wan.	2
Round 3	Mansfield Town	2	Peterborough United	2
	Mansfield Town won 3-1 on penalties.			
Round 3	Port Vale	2	Sutton United	1
Round 3	Salford City	0	Burnley	4
Round 3	Manchester United	3	Crystal Palace	0
Round 3	Aston Villa	1	Everton	2
Round 3	Blackburn Rovers	5	Cardiff City	2
Round 3	Bournemouth	2	Stoke City	0
Round 3	Brentford	0	Arsenal	1
Round 3	Chelsea	1	Brighton & Hove Albion	0
Round 3	Fulham	2	Norwich City	1
Round 3	Lincoln City	0	West Ham United	1
Round 3	Liverpool	3	Leicester City	1
Round 3	Newcastle United	1	Manchester City	0
Round 4	Exeter City	2	Middlesbrough	3
Round 4	Mansfield Town	0	Port Vale	1
Round 4	West Ham United	3	Arsenal	1
Round 4	Bournemouth	1	Liverpool	2

Round 4	Chelsea	2	Blackburn Rovers	0	
Round 4	Everton	3	Burnley	0	
Round 4	Iipswich Town	1	Fulham	3	
Round 4	Manchester United	0	Newcastle United	3	
Round 5	Everton	1	Fulham	1	
	Fulham won 7-6 on penalties.				
Round 5	Port Vale	0	Middlesbrough	3	
Round 5	Chelsea	1	Newcastle United	1	
	Chelsea won 4-2 on penalties.				
Round 5	Liverpool	5	West Ham United	1	
Semi-finals					
1st leg	Middlesbrough	1	Chelsea	0	
1st leg	Liverpool	2	Fulham	1	
2nd leg	Chelsea	6	Middlesbrough	1	
	Chelsea won 6-2 on aggregate.				
2nd leg	Fulham	1	Liverpool	1	
	Liverpool won 3-2 on aggregate.				
FINAL	Liverpool	1	Chelsea	0	(aet)

112

9th September 2023
v UKRAINE (ECQ)   *Wroclaw*

J. Pickford	Everton
K. Walker	Manchester City
M. Guèhi	Crystal Palace
H. Maguire	Manchester United
B. Chilwell	Chelsea
J. Bellingham	Real Madrid (sub. P. Foden 66)
D. Rice	Arsenal
J. Henderson	Al-Ettifaq
B. Saka	Arsenal (sub. C. Gallagher 87)
H. Kane	Bayern Munich
J. Maddison	Tottenham H. (sub. M. Rashford 66)

Result 1-1   Walker

12th September 2023
v SCOTLAND   *Hampden Park*

A. Ramsdale	Arsenal
K. Walker	Manchester United
K. Trippier	Newcastle United
D. Rice	Arsenal
M. Guèhi	Crystal Palace (sub. H. Maguire 45)
L. Dunk	Brighton & Hove Albion
P. Foden	Manchester City (sub. B. Saka 71)
K. Phillips	Manchester City
H. Kane	Bayern Munich (sub. C. Wilson 84)
J. Bellingham	Real Madrid (sub. C. Gallagher 84)
M. Rashford	Manchester United (sub. E. Eze 71)

Result 3-1   Foden, Bellingham, Kane

13th October 2023
v AUSTRALIA   *Wembley*

S. Johnstone	Crystal Palace
T. Alexander-Arnold	Liverpool
L. Colwill	Chelsea
C. Gallagher	Chelsea (sub. K. Phillips 61)
L. Dunk	Brighton and Hove Albion
F. Tomori	AC Milan (sub. J. Stones 61)
J. Grealish	Man. City (sub. M. Rashford 61)
J. Henderson	Al-Ettifaq (sub. K. Trippier 61)
O. Watkins	Aston Villa (sub. E. Nketiah 72)
J. Maddison	Tottenham Hot. (sub. P. Foden 72)
J. Bowen	West Ham United

Result 1-0   Watkins

17th October 2023
v ITALY (ECQ)   *Wembley*

J. Pickford	Everton
K. Walker	Manchester City
K. Trippier	Newcastle United
D. Rice	Arsenal
J. Stones	Manchester City (sub. M. Guehi 63)
H. Maguire	Manchester United
P. Foden	Manchester City
K. Phillips	Man. City (sub. J. Henderson 69)
H. Kane	Bayern Munich
J. Bellingham	Real Madrid (sub. J. Grealish 85)
M. Rashford	Manchester United

Result 3-1   Kane 2 (1 pen), Rashford

17th November 2023
v MALTA (ECQ)   *Wembley*

J. Pickford	Everton
K. Trippier	Newcastle United
F. Tomori	AC Milan (sub. B. Saka 46)
C. Gallagher	Chelsea (sub. K. Walker 46)
M. Guèhi	Crystal Palace
H. Maguire	Manchester United
P. Foden	Manchester City
J. Henderson	Al-Ettifaq (sub. D. Rice 61)
H. Kane	Bayern Munich
T. Alexander-Arnold	Liverpool
M. Rashford	Man. United (sub. C. Palmer 61)

Result 2-0   Pepe (o.g.), Kane

20th November 2023
v North Macedonia (ECQ)   *Skopje*

J. Pickford	Everton
K. Walker	Manchester City
R. Lewis	Manchester City
D. Rice	Arsenal
M. Guèhi	Crystal Palace
H. Maguire	Manchester United
B. Saka	Arsenal (sub. C. Palmer 84)
P. Foden	Manchester City
O. Watkins	Aston Villa (sub. H. Kane 58)
T. Alexander-Arnold	Liverpool (sub. K. Phillips 84)
J. Grealish	Man. City (sub. M. Rashford 84)

Result 1-1   Atanasov (o.g.)

ENGLAND INTERNATIONAL LINE-UPS AND STATISTICS 2024

23rd March 2024
v BRAZIL *Wembley*

J. Pickford	Everton
K. Walker	Manchester City (sub. E. Konsa 28)
B. Chilwell	Chelsea (sub. J. Gomez 67)
D. Rice	Arsenal
J. Stones	Manchester City
H. Maguire	Manchester United
P. Foden	Manchester City
C. Gallagher	Chelsea (sub. K. Mainoo 75)
O. Watkins	Aston Villa
J. Bellingham	Real Madrid (sub. J. Bowen 67)
A. Gordon	Newcastle Utd. (sub. M. Rashford 75)

Result 0-1

26th March 2024
v BELGIUM *Wembley*

J. Pickford	Everton
E. Konsa	Aston Villa
B. Chilwell	Chelsea
D. Rice	Arsenal
J. Stones	Manchester City (sub. J. Gomez 10)
L. Dunk	Brighton & Hove Albion
P. Foden	Manchester City
J. Bellingham	Real Madrid
I. Toney	Brentford (sub. O. Watkins 80)
J. Bowen	West Ham United (sub. A. Gordon 80)
K. Mainoo	Man. United (sub. J. Maddison 74)

Result 2-2 Toney (pen), Bellingham

3rd June 2024
v BOSNIA & HERZEGOVINA *Newcastle*

J. Pickford	Everton
K. Trippier	Newcastle Utd. (sub. A. Wharton 62)
E. Konsa	Aston Villa (sub. J. Gomez 73)
C. Gallagher	Chelsea
L. Dunk	Brighton & Hove Albion
M. Guèhi	Crystal Pal. (sub. J. Branthwaite 62)
C. Palmer	Chelsea (sub. J. Grealish 62)
T. Alexander-Arnold	Liverpool
O. Watkins	Aston Villa (sub. H. Kane 61)
E. Eze	Crystal Palace
J. Bowen	West Ham United

Result 3-0 Palmer, Alexander-Arnold, Kane

7th June 2024
v ICELAND *Wembley*

A. Ramsdale	Arsenal
K. Walker	Man. City (sub. T. Alexander-Arnold 64)
K. Trippier	Newcastle United (sub. J. Gomez 64)
D. Rice	Arsenal
J. Stones	Manchester City (sub. E. Konsa 46)
M. Guèhi	Crystal Palace
C. Palmer	Chelsea (sub. E. Eze 77)
K. Mainoo	Manchester United
H. Kane	Bayern Munich (sub. I. Toney 64)
P. Foden	Manchester City
A. Gordon	Newcastle United (sub. A. Gordon 64)

Result 0-1

16th June 2024
v SERBIA (EC) *Gelsenkirchen*

J. Pickford	Everton
K. Walker	Manchester City
D. Rice	Arsenal
J. Stones	Manchester City
M. Guèhi	Crystal Palace
B. Saka	Arsenal (sub. J. Bowen 76)
T. Alexander-Arnold	Liverpool (sub. C. Gallagher 69)
H. Kane	Bayern Munich
J. Bellingham	Real Madrid (K. Mainoo 86)
P. Foden	Manchester City
K. Trippier	Newcastle United

Result 1-0 Bellingham

20th June 2024
v DENMARK (EC) *Frankfurt*

J. Pickford	Everton
K. Walker	Manchester City
D. Rice	Arsenal
J. Stones	Manchester City
M. Guèhi	Crystal Palace
B. Saka	Arsenal (sub. E. Eze 69)
T. Alexander-Arnold	Liverpool (sub. C. Gallagher 54)
H. Kane	Bayern Munich (sub. O. Watkins 69)
J. Bellingham	Real Madrid
P. Foden	Manchester City (sub. J. Bowen 69)
K. Trippier	Newcastle United

Result 1-1 Kane

25th June 2024
v SLOVENIA *Cologne*

J. Pickford	Everton
K. Walker	Manchester City
D. Rice	Arsenal
J. Stones	Manchester City
M. Guèhi	Crystal Palace
B. Saka	Arsenal (sub. C. Palmer 71)
H. Kane	Bayern Munich
J. Bellingham	Real Madrid
P. Foden	Manchester City (sub. A. Gordon 89)
K. Trippier	Newcastle Utd (sub. T. Alexander-Arnold 85)
C. Gallagher	Chelsea (sub. K. Mainoo 46)

Result 0-0

30th June 2024
v SLOVAKIA (EC) *Gelsenkirchen*

J. Pickford	Everton
K. Walker	Manchester City
D. Rice	Arsenal
J. Stones	Manchester City
M. Guèhi	Crystal Palace
B. Saka	Arsenal
H. Kane	Bayern Mun. (sub. C. Gallagher 105)
J. Bellingham	Real Madrid (sub. E. Konsa 105)
P. Foden	Manchester City (sub. I. Toney 90+5)
K. Trippier	Newcastle United (sub. C. Palmer 66)
K. Mainoo	Manchester United (sub. E. Eze 84)

Result 2-1 Bellingham, Kane

6th June 2024
v SWITZERLAND (EC) *Dusseldorf*

Jordan Pickford	Everton
Kyle Walker	Manchester City
Declan Rice	Arsenal
John Stones	Manchester City
Bukayo Saka	Arsenal
Harry Kane	Bayern Munich (sub. I. Toney 109)
Jude Bellingham	Real Madrid
Phil Foden	Man. City (sub. T. Alexander-Arnold 115)
Kieran Trippier	Newcastle United (sub. L. Shaw 78)
Ezri Konsa	Aston Villa (sub. E. Eze 78)
Kobbie Mainoo	Man. United (sub. C. Palmer 78)

Result 1-1 Saka
England won 5-3 on penalties.

10th July 2024
v NETHERLANDS (EC) *Dortmund*

J. Pickford	Everton
K. Walker	Manchester City
D. Rice	Arsenal
J. Stones	Manchester City
M. Guèhi	Crystal Palace
B. Saka	Arsenal (sub. E. Konsa 90+3)
H. Kane	Bayern Munich (sub. O. Watkins 80)
J. Bellingham	Real Madrid
P. Foden	Manchester City (sub. C. Palmer 80)
K. Trippier	Newcastle United (sub. L. Shaw 46)
K. Mainoo	Man. United (sub. C. Gallagher 90+3)

Result 2-1 Kane, Watkins

14th July 2024
v SPAIN (EC FINAL) *Berlin*

J. Pickford	Everton
K. Walker	Manchester City
L. Shaw	Manchester United
D. Rice	Arsenal
J. Stones	Manchester City
M. Guèhi	Crystal Palace
B. Saka	Arsenal
H. Kane	Bayern Munich (sub. O. Watkins 61)
J. Bellingham	Real Madrid
P. Foden	Manchester City (sub. I. Toney 89)
K. Mainoo	Man. United (sub. C. Palmer 70)

Result 1-2 Palmer